Pedagogies for Equitable Access

A volume in
*Teacher Education in Global Contexts:
Promoting Culturally Sustaining Teachers and Teacher Educators*
Luciana C. de Oliveira and Yaoying Xu, *Series Editors*

Pedagogies for Equitable Access

Reimagining Multilingual Education for an Uncertain World

edited by

Lourdes Cardozo-Gaibisso
Mississippi State University

Ruth Harman
University of Georgia

Max Vazquez Dominguez
University of North Georgia

Cory Buxton
Oregon State University

INFORMATION AGE PUBLISHING, INC.
Charlotte, NC • www.infoagepub.com

Library of Congress Cataloging-in-Publication Data

A CIP record for this book is available from the Library of Congress
http://www.loc.gov

ISBN: 979-8-88730-744-2 (Paperback)
       979-8-88730-745-9 (Hardcover)
       979-8-88730-746-6 (E-Book)

Copyright © 2024 Information Age Publishing Inc.

All rights reserved. No part of this publication may be reproduced, stored in a retrieval system, or transmitted, in any form or by any means, electronic, mechanical, photocopying, microfilming, recording or otherwise, without written permission from the publisher.

Printed in the United States of America

CONTENTS

Foreword vii
Magdalena Pando

1 Competencies Applied to Teaching an ESOL Methods Course
 Moved to the Online Environment... 1
 Luciana C. de Oliveira and Larisa Olesova

2 How Emergency Remote Online Language Teaching
 Informed Post-Lockdown Language Teaching Practices:
 The Case of Two Chinese EFL Elementary Teachers 17
 Carla Meskill, Dongni Guo, Fang Wang, and Wuri Kusumastuti

3 Exploring New Assessment Scenarios During the Pandemic:
 The Case for Design-Based Research 39
 Gabriel Díaz Maggioli

4 Flexibility in Teaching During the Pandemic: An Action-
 Research Study of a University Foreign Language Classroom.......... 57
 María Eugenia Lozano

5 Navigating Complexity: Fostering Inclusive Social
 Environments in Bilingual Education Through
 Multimodal Communication.. 77
 *Wilder Yesid Escobar-Almeciga, Lorena Caviedes-Cadena,
 and Fabián Benavides Jiménez*

6 Comparing Elementary School Teachers' Culturally
  Responsive Practices in China and the United States During
  and Beyond the COVID-19 Pandemic 95
  Alicia R. Thompson and Yaoying Xu

7 Mapping a Multilingual Future: Navigating Uncertainty
  With Equitable Pedagogies 113
  *Lourdes Cardozo-Gaibisso, Ruth Harman, Max Vazquez Dominguez,
  and Cory Buxton*

About the Contributors 119

FOREWORD

Without question the coronavirus pandemic transformed education on a global scale as mass movement from in-person teaching shifted to online teaching. The year 2020 reminds us how the pandemic induced a pedagogical breakthrough which presently continues to transform the field of education as ever-evolving policies and technologies emerge. In this series, K–12 researchers, teacher educators and policy makers, provide readers with insightful perspectives and advancements in effective teaching practices, innovative pedagogies, and theoretical perspectives to provide access to student learning and success. The research-centered agendas of the authors exemplify adaptability, flexibility, navigation, and innovation, which are paramount for equitable teaching. The chapters that follow exemplify research on instructional strategy use and curriculum adaptations, teacher education practices, and classroom-based pedagogical innovations and assessment. The ingenuity of the researchers authoring these chapters invite readers to reimagine, assessment practices, bilingual teacher education programs, methods and research for teaching English to speakers of other languages (ESOL), English as a foreign language, Spanish as foreign language, and multilingual-multicultural teacher education.

The contributors of this edited volume employ a wide range of research methodologies to reimagine multilingual education. These include qualitative case studies, design-based research, self-study, action-based research, video-cued ethnography and theory-based perspectives. Researchers illuminate the path forward, showcasing not only the challenges they have overcome as educators, but also the opportunities and affordances they have seized to enhance student engagement and achievement through their research and practice. This collection underscores the transformative power of reflective practice and professional development in shaping the future of education. The effect of the pandemic is forever more present in education, and contributors share their research to demonstrate adaptations and innovation in pedagogy for increasing access and opportunity in language education.

In Chapter 1, de Oliveira and Olesova, present readers with a self-study on a post-secondary course about methods for teaching English to speakers of other languages (ESOL) which shifted from a face-to-face modality to an online environment during the pandemic. Through self-study design the authors promote both teaching as reflection and knowledge development through reflective practice. They present readers with instructor competencies in teaching to adapt practice from in-person teaching and explain model practices in an online instructional modality that facilitates student engagement and interaction. Findings from the ESOL teacher educator's self-study highlight the importance of building community through effective communication, modeling instructor presence, dedicating structured time to reflect and develop knowledge about online instructional methodologies and technologies, setting online expectations, and creating collaborative synchronous and asynchronous activities and assignment in the course. The authors offer a comprehensive approach to self-study design to offer valuable guidance for educators to create equitable access to enhance student engagement and interaction in online environments.

In Chapter 2, Meskill and colleagues present readers with a longitudinal qualitative case study of two Chinese elementary teachers who shift between in-person and online teaching spaces while teaching English as a foreign language (EFL) during the pandemic. The authors underscore the affordance of interactivity strategies during the pandemic lockdown and post-lockdown. They examine interactivity through four dimensions. First, teacher-student interactivity strategies consisted of using digital video-recorded mini-lessons to offer learning and teaching efficiency and found that the use of these improved student outcomes. Secondly, parents and students created digital products (e.g., audio/video recordings) to share as resources in their online learning space with other students. By teachers encouraging parents to take on the role of supervisors, facilitators and learning partners, parents helped regulate students' emotions while supporting them through learning tasks and assignments. Thirdly, teachers' questioning during synchronous activities and assignment of digital homework through the use of digital applications created spaces for online praising and motivating students. Finally, student to student interaction occurred through the creation of WeChat groups where students worked collaboratively. Meskill and colleagues share implications for continued use of technology applications, peer mediation through technology and parent/family support to address the needs of students while creating spaces for interaction and access to learning.

In Chapter 3, Díaz Maggioli suggests the use of design-based research (DBR) as a methodology in which pre-service teachers, their subject-matter teaching and learning instructor, and cooperating teacher navigate assessment practices in student teaching field experiences in Uruguay. The researcher presents readers with a student teacher-centered DBR project to design an intervention in teacher education. The intervention focuses on the assessment of communication skills, while teaching English as a foreign language (EFL) and considers both the pre-service teachers' and students' needs. Design-based research helped pre-service teachers identify concerns and needs in their field experience, and also helped them consider those of their students to design an intervention for assessing communication skills, test the intervention and reflect on the results and its continued change towards improvement.

In Chapter 4, Lozano presents an action-research study of a post-secondary course where Spanish is taught as a foreign language at an institution of higher education. The author features the need to redesign the assessment component of the Spanish language program in undergraduate language education. She details how program faculty formed a committee to shift from summative mid-term and final assessments to formative assessments referred to as "unit wrap-ups." The change from summative to formative assessment revealed a positive experience for both students and faculty in the language learning program. Faculty felt there was no pressure for "covering" material before exams as students knew specifically what they would be assessed on, thereby reducing anxiety. Students expressed preferring more assessments throughout the semester over a midterm and final exam. Lozano encourages educators to embrace flexibility by modifying assignments and assessments to better meet the needs of students, creating a sense of shared responsibility versus the instructor being the sole authority in class.

In Chapter 5, Escobar-Almeciga and colleagues offer theory-based reflections about a bilingual teaching program while shifting from in-classroom communication and migration into technology-mediated spaces. The authors offer conceptual framings for teaching English as a foreign language (EFL) by recognizing the role of interaction as a system of intricate relationships for meaning-making in an EFL social climate. The researchers stress striving for learning-conducive social environments that promote communication, interaction, active participation and collaboration in a bilingual teaching program, while considering ethical concerns about equitable communication opportunities for bilingualism in the classroom.

In Chapter 6, Thompson and Xu employ video-cued ethnography and culture circles to explore cultural responsiveness in elementary school teachers in China and the United States. The researchers highlight comparisons in two global contexts to recommend the significance of implementing school-based culture circles which encourage teachers' questioning of current realities and leverage existing knowledge, fostering community and family partnerships, and address gaps in evidence-based practices to increase their own knowledge of multicultural education and culturally responsive teaching. Using video-cued ethnography the researchers prompted teachers to reflect about their own practice to share insights about their interactions with students. Using culture circles the researchers examined the culturally relevant teaching practice perceptions of teachers from both countries. Video recordings prompted discussions stressing the need to foster positive perspectives on parents and families, set high expectations, learning within the context of culture, use student-centered instruction, leverage culturally-mediated instruction, reshape the curriculum, and practice as facilitator to increase access for students.

At its core, this collection underscores the transformative power of reflective practice and professional development in shaping the future of education. As we embark on this journey of discovery and growth, technological advances, policy and curricular reform, let us draw inspiration from the experiences and research findings shared to reaffirm our commitment to excellence in language teaching and learning. May the wisdom contained herein inform and inspire your own pedagogical endeavors, enriching the lives of students and educators alike.

—Magdalena Pando, PhD
Associate Professor
Department of Teaching & Learning
Simmons School of Education & Human Development
Southern Methodist University

CHAPTER 1

COMPETENCIES APPLIED TO TEACHING AN ESOL METHODS COURSE MOVED TO THE ONLINE ENVIRONMENT

Luciana C. de Oliveira
Virginia Commonwealth University

Larisa Olesova
College of Education, University of Florida

ABSTRACT

This self-study shares instructor competencies based on adaptations made to a face-to-face ESL method course that was moved to the online environment due to the COVID-19 pandemic. Specifically, this self-study explores how these competencies were expressed in one specific course to explain model practices to facilitate engagement and interactions in asynchronous online learning.

Online learning became a reality for university professors and students as a consequence of the COVID-19 pandemic in 2020. This shift from face-to-face to online environments was sudden and unexpected. Adaptations to content, assignments, and delivery formats became necessary. Teaching and learning in this new environment present increased responsibilities, challenges, and opportunities to improve existing competencies. Competencies that specify the required skills, attitudes, and knowledge of a competent instructor for face-to-face, online, and blended settings have been identified in the literature and used to provide standards for best practices (Grabowski et al., 2016; Klein et al., 2004; Martin, Budhrani, Kumar & Ritzhaupt, 2019). These competencies are divided into five domains: professional foundations, planning and preparation, instructional methods and strategies, assessment and evaluation, and management. Though these competencies are not specific to any field, they can be used to explore the knowledge and skills needed to move from face-to-face teaching environments to online.

In teaching English to speakers of other languages (TESOL), methods courses are commonly taught to prepare pre-service teachers to work with an increasing population of multilingual learners (MLs). These students speak languages other than English in K–12 schools. These courses can be taught face-to-face, online, or hybrid. When the COVID-19 pandemic started in March 2020, many methods courses had to be moved to the online environment quickly and swiftly. This was the case with the experience we report on in this chapter.

This chapter explores specific instructor competencies based on adaptations made to a face-to-face ESOL Methods course that was moved to the online environment due to the COVID-19 pandemic. This self-study uses examples of practice to show how these competencies were expressed in this course and explain how these constitute model practices for online learning to facilitate engagement and interaction.

COMPETENCIES FOR FACE-TO-FACE, ONLINE, AND BLENDED SETTINGS

The field of teacher education has long seen a focus on competencies necessary for teachers in various areas (Albanese et al., 2008; Field, 1979). Competencies are defined as dynamic and complex elements and actions that combine attitudes, skills, and knowledge to guide effective performance (Carraccio et al., 2002; O'Flaherty & Beal, 2018). Well established in the education literature is the importance of a knowledge base for teaching, including knowledge of the subject, general pedagogical knowledge, pedagogical content knowledge, curriculum knowledge, educational context knowledge, and knowledge of learners and their contexts (Shulman, 1987).

Knowledge is demonstrated through teachers' performance and actions in the field. Teaching practices are critical to teacher development; teachers apply knowledge and skills in classrooms as they continue to improve and learn (Ball & Forzani, 2010).

Studies have discussed whether instructor competencies differ between face-to-face, online, and blended settings (Creasman, 2014; Wang et al., 2021). We agree that the competencies required for online and blended teaching should be perceived differently from those in face-to-face settings (Zou et al., 2021). We believe that when instructors are separated from their students in terms of space or time, requirements for teaching competencies are more complex and include the need for technological competence (Thomas & Graham, 2019). Technological competence includes the ability to use the learning management system (LMS) to design and teach the course and other technology skills (E-mail, navigating browser windows, file upload and download, and PDF creation) as both primary and essential for online teaching (Martin, Budhrani, Kumar, & Ritzhaupt, 2019). Other technology skills include the ability to create and upload videos, use tools for screencasts, record with a microphone and voice-over with PowerPoint, and use a webcam to help students learn, that is, provide audio or video feedback, create additional support materials and others (Martin, Budhrani, Kumar, & Ritzhaupt, 2019; Olesova & de Oliveira, 2015). When instructors ignore differences between online/blended and face-to-face teaching, they deliver their lectures online without thoughtful planning of online learning experiences.

It should be noted that thoughtfully planned online learning differs from online learning offered in response to the COVID-19 pandemic. Emergency remote teaching (ERT) during the COVID-19 pandemic has temporarily shifted instructional delivery to an alternative delivery mode due to crisis circumstances (Hodges et al., 2020). ERT involves using fully remote teaching solutions for instruction that would otherwise be delivered face-to-face and that return to that format once the emergency has abated (Hodges et al., 2020).

Thomas and Graham (2019) recommended developing a more comprehensive model of online teaching competencies. The authors stated that online instructors should be evaluated based on their instructional behaviors (facilitation) rather than the course design. By emphasizing the following instructional behaviors, such as the ability to build relationships and community with and among students, to adapt to students' diverse needs, and to connect students to course content in relevant and personalized ways, authors stated that these types of behavior can help students be successful in an online course. Moreover, when evaluating instructional behaviors, this approach should help institutions provide more focused and timely training and professional development. On the contrary, Martin, Budhrani, Kumar, and Ritzhaupt (2019) emphasized the importance of course design competencies when teaching professional development programs are designed online. However, when Martin, Budhrani, and

TABLE 1.1 Domains and Competencies (Grabowski et al., 2016; Klein et al., 2004; Martin et al., 2019)

Domain	Competencies
Professional Foundations	• Effective communication • Improvement of professional knowledge and skills • Compliance with ethical and legal standards • Maintenance of professional credibility
Planning and Preparation	• Planning of methods and materials • Preparation for instruction
Instructional Methods and Strategies	• Continuation of learner motivation and engagement • Demonstration of effective presentation skills • Demonstration of effective facilitation skills • Demonstration of effective questioning skills • Delivery of clarification and feedback • Promotion of retention of knowledge and skills • Promotion of transfer of knowledge and skills • Use of media and technology to enhance learning and performance
Assessment and Evaluation	• Assessment of learning and performance • Evaluation of instructional effectiveness
Management	• Management of an environment that fosters learning and performance • Management of the instructional process through the appropriate use of technology

Wang (2019) discussed the course design, the authors mentioned the importance of the instructor's focus on engaging learners through designing online learning activities that facilitate the learning process. Moreover, the authors also mentioned that learning activities should provide opportunities for interaction due to the distance between students and the time they spend online. It seems that their vision is close to what Thomas and Graham (2019) argued that instructors should be evaluated by their facilitation competence because many institutions utilize a master course model where the course instructor is not responsible for course design.

Faculty who engage in online teaching and learning generally need to develop specific competencies for working effectively in online contexts. Competencies that specify the required skills, attitudes, and knowledge of a competent instructor for face-to-face, online, and blended settings have been identified in the literature and used to provide standards for best practices (Grabowski et al., 2016; Table 1.1).

METHOD

Self-study is a robust methodology for identifying the competencies used by a teacher educator in moving from face-to-face to online teaching.

Self-studies focus on teacher educators' practice and allow for exploring a pedagogy of teacher education. How a self-study might be done depends on what is sought to be better understood (Pinnegar, 1998). Learning through self-study enables us to develop an articulated knowledge about practice and question this knowledge through systematic investigation. Self-study researchers aim to explore and identify their professional expertise to advance the knowledge base of teacher education (Loughran, 2005, 2007). As such, research questions "are embedded in teacher educators' real concerns and dilemmas within their practice" (Nilsson & Loughran, 2012, p. 122). As self-study participants, we look at "one's self, one's actions, one's ideas" (Hamilton & Pinnegar, 1998, p. 236). Self-study researchers may use existing written data such as lesson plans, comments on discussion boards, and syllabi, not necessarily collecting new data as part of their investigation (Vanassche & Kelchtermans, 2015).

Self-study promotes the idea of teaching as reflection and the development of knowledge through reflective practice. It models an inquiry-based approach to pedagogy by providing opportunities for teachers at all levels to reflect on teaching and learning and generate rich understandings of their practice. Because self-study involves inquiring into a teacher educator's professional experiences to improve their practice, this methodology provides opportunities for reflecting upon, critically analyzing, and evaluating practice (Pinnegar & Hamilton, 2009).

We chose to engage in a self-study since it allowed us to examine Luciana's practices in moving to the online environment and understanding practice problems specifically (Dinkelman, 2003). An essential aspect of this self-study was the desire to understand better the competencies that a teacher educator used during the pandemic. Thus, the data we used were specifically chosen to reach that goal. Though the focus of analysis is on Luciana's practices, we follow from the finding that collaboration with a trusted colleague is a robust approach as we consider different interpretations of collected data (Fletcher & Bullock, 2012). Therefore, Larisa engages in this self-study as a critical friend and trusted colleague with expertise in online teaching and learning. Next, we detail the steps we followed during data collection and analysis.

Data Collection and Analysis

Luciana reflected on the implementation of activities, especially considering the domains identified in the literature: Professional foundations, planning and preparation, instructional methods and strategies, assessment and evaluation, and management. Course syllabus, content, organization, activities, discussions, and assessments were used as data to identify the competencies used to move the course online.

We engaged in interpretive qualitative analysis (e.g., Cochran-Smith & Lytle, 2004; Creswell, 2009) using the constant comparative method (Corbin & Strauss, 2014) to explore the data and identify initial themes as they related to competencies identified in the research literature. To identify initial themes, we began by working independently to explore the data, including course materials, online posts, and feedback on students' lesson plans. Next, we looked more carefully at the organization of the course online, information about each module, online tasks, and additional information provided by Luciana throughout the course. After carefully examining the data, we identified the domain of instructional methods and strategies to explore further as the course focused on methods for teaching MLs. However, we present results for all domains.

The ESOL Methods Course

This ESOL methods course was entitled "ESOL Methods, Curriculum, and Assessments." It was taught at South University (pseudonym) in Spring 2020. The course description read:

> This course addresses the application of TESOL theories, principles, and current research to the use of curriculum, methods, and assessment. In doing so, the course focuses on an understanding of the differences between curriculum, methods, and assessments designed for children who are proficient speakers of English and those designed for ESOL services. Specific TESOL modifications appropriate for content areas are also addressed. Field experience required. This course counts as the second of two required ESOL-specific courses. Advanced written proficiencies are emphasized in this course as part of the Upper-Level Communication Requirement (UCLR).

Activities included field experience, project-based assignments, collaborative interaction, and lecture and discussion. The course was divided into three modules, with specific weeks dedicated to each, which made it much easier to move to the online environment. The modules were:

Module 1: Introduction to ESOL Methods, Curriculum and Assessment
Module 2: Planning and Assessing Curriculum for Emergent Bilinguals: The Four Skills
Module 3: Integration in Teaching and Learning the Content Areas

Module 1 lasted 4 weeks and introduced students to some basic concepts that were to be developed later on in the class, including terminology in the field; disproportionate representation of emergent bilinguals in special education; identification and assessment of emergent bilinguals; assessment, programs, and policies for serving emergent bilinguals; high challenge, high support classrooms; and standards and assessment. Module 2 covered more specific topics related to teaching what is commonly known in TESOL as "the four skills": scaffolding language and learning; classroom talk; from speaking to writing; writing in a second language; reading in a second language; listening in a second language; assessing oral proficiency and literacy development; and assessment *as, for,* and *of* learning. Module 3 was more related to integrating content and language learning with topics such as teaching activities for an integrated curriculum, engaging emergent bilinguals in content area instruction (science and mathematics), and engaging emergent bilinguals in content area instruction (social studies and ELA/literacy).

The course moved online just as the class was finishing up Module 2. This is important to include here because most of the course's key concepts had been developed by the students face-to-face, forming a good foundation for the continuation of the content online.

The course included a variety of assignments and assessments. Critical assessments with their corresponding points are presented in Table 1.2.

As can be seen, much weight was placed on the lesson plan, assessment design project, and the abridged research paper. The lesson plan project was an essential part of the course, as students had a chance to plan instruction using the content and strategies they learned throughout the course. The abridged research paper had recently been integrated into this course to fulfill the university writing communication requirement. This assessment gave students an opportunity to explore a specific topic they had learned about in the course in more depth.

TABLE 1.2 Key Assessments and Points

Requirement	Points
1. Class Attendance and Active Participation	15
2. Part 1 of Lesson Plan and Assessment Design Project	15
3. Part 2 of Lesson Plan and Assessment Design Project	30
3. First Draft of Abridged Research Paper	25
4. Final Draft of Abridged Research Paper	15
TOTAL (100%)	**100**

FINDINGS AND DISCUSSION

For each domain and competencies, we identify examples from practice from our data set that are closely connected to the domain and competencies.

Domain 1: Professional Foundations

This domain includes the following competencies: *Effective communication, improvement of professional knowledge and skills, compliance with ethical and legal standards,* and *maintenance of professional credibility.* In terms of effective communication, Luciana used multiple means to communicate with students. She used the learning management system (LMS, i.e., Blackboard) to provide announcements each week with major assignment due dates. Email within the LMS and regular email from the university were used as points of contact. In addition, as soon as the course was moved online, she started a GroupMe group with the students which she used to clarify expectations, to remind students of deadlines, and to answer students' questions. Students used GroupMe to communicate with one another as well about collaborative projects and continued using this tool to ask questions from one another as well. GroupMe was particularly effective since it does not require participants to share their phone numbers—you simply create a group and send it to students for them to become members of the group, then after the course was over, the group was deleted. In addition, synchronous individual and group sessions (e.g., Zoom) were used at least once a week for the remainder of the semester (7 weeks out of a 15-week schedule) which expanded the instructor's social presence and enabled students to communicate concerns and questions as everyone was adapting to the new format of course delivery.

Another competency apparent from the data was *improvement of professional knowledge and skills.* One example was her expansion of knowledge related to online instructional strategies through readings and professional learning. Luciana sought out opportunities to grow in pedagogy and technology skills while she was moving the course online (personal reflection, April 2020). She allocated time each week to learn more about online learning and how to teach online by reading relevant research she could find, including Cavanaugh (2005), Crawford-Ferre and Wiest (2012), Fish and Wickersham (2009), and Major (2015).

For *compliance with ethical and legal standards,* we noticed specifically compliance with professional code of ethics and fair treatment of students in difficult situations as examples. Luciana sought out to develop knowledge of web accessibility regulations to understand what needed to be done in relation to adaptations necessary for students, if they indeed were needed.

She also sought to understand students' educational, academic, and personal circumstances as the pandemic had just started. Five of the 12 students in the class had returned to their home states and three reported having low bandwidth for their Internet connection, making things difficult for learning online. Yet, they persevered and completed the course successfully. Luciana provided several extensions to class assignments due to unforeseen circumstances for students. This connects back to the competency of communication as a critical component of online teaching and learning. Students and instructors communicated constantly in order to solve issues and address challenges that the pandemic presented.

Maintenance of professional credibility included demonstration of subject-matter expertise and exemplary professional conduct, demonstrated by Luciana as an expert in the field, with a strong knowledge base of the subject matter, understanding of the content in TESOL to be able to deliver it effectively for learners, and pedagogical content knowledge to be able to address the needs of pre-service teachers. Specifically, Luciana had over 25 years of teaching experience in the field of TESOL, had been a secondary ESOL teacher, and had been a researcher in TESOL for 15 years at the time of this course. In addition, the year prior to when the course was taught, she served as president of the largest international association for ESOL teachers, TESOL International Association.

Domain 2: Planning and Preparation

Within this domain, *planning of methods and materials* and *preparation for instruction* were identified as competencies. For the competency *planning of methods and materials*, the following examples of practice were observed: selection of appropriate instructional strategies; incorporation of collaborative, social learning activities; and modifications to the schedule, lessons, and evaluation tools

Our data show how Luciana modified instruction to accommodate students' various needs and new instructional formats. Because she developed an understanding of how students learn in synchronous and asynchronous modes, she used strategies for interaction through assignments that integrated collaborative activities and interactions through the discussion board and other interactive activities. One assignment entitled "Leading of a Discussion Session" was particularly noteworthy. The assignment consisted of two parts. For Part A, entitled "Summary, Analysis, and Discussion Question," students were responsible for summarizing the article/chapter they had read for that week. They focused their analysis on the content and implications of the article/chapter and included how it related to teaching MLs. Students wrote a one-page summary and analysis of the article/

chapter. This was a group assignment, so Luciana suggested using Google Docs so they could do this in groups. In addition, students had to create a discussion question (DQ) based on the article/chapter. Luciana provided examples of good discussion questions. Students were to submit the (a) one-page article summary and analysis, and (b) DQ based on the article/chapter by Monday at 9:00 p.m. of the week the reading of that article/chapter was scheduled. Part B, "Responding to Postings and Writing a Summary," was for the week that particular group was leading the discussion. Students were responsible for:

1. replying to at least 2 postings from students (2 per person in the group);
2. writing a summary of the weekly postings that included the most interesting, informative, and/or relevant points made by the group in order to conclude the week. The summary was posted by Monday at 6 pm of the week after the discussion.

This assignment was a highlight of the course for students as they felt it was an excellent and shared way to engage with the course content. Incorporation of collaborative, social learning activities and use of collaborative technologies are essential for students' engagement online. They did not feel overwhelmed by the discussions because they had clear learning objectives.

Every Monday of each week, Luciana included a one to two-page document that explicitly stated the learning objectives for the week, the assignments that were due, and the discussion question for the week. These documents with explicit information were fundamental for students to understand what needed to be done for the week and overall the expectations for the course.

In terms of *preparation for instruction,* Luciana used flexible learning models that accommodated diverse learning needs. She created additional materials for students experiencing difficulties, communicated with them as they expressed confusion about assignments or issues and clarified expectations. This was extremely important for the success of the course (personal reflection, May 2020). In addition, she used relevant examples and additional materials needed by developing a mix of activities for various ways of learning (e.g., social vs. individual, oral vs. visual), and adjusted instruction and evaluation tools based on student feedback.

Domain 3: Instructional Methods and Strategies

For Domain 3, the following competencies have been identified: *continuation of learner motivation and engagement; demonstration of effective presentation, facilitation, and questioning skills; delivery of clarification and feedback; promotion of retention and transfer of knowledge and skills;* and *use of media and technology to enhance learning and performance.*

It is important to provide opportunities for all learners to participate and be engaged in multiple ways. The activities developed for the ESOL Methods course expected students to engage with the course content and share their understanding and knowledge developed through course readings. One of the documents we examined was entitled "Expectations: Moving to the Online Environment." This document contained critical information for students as they were getting used to the course being online for the remaining seven weeks of the semester. The document was subdivided into sections that included the following headings and subheadings:

ASSIGNMENTS AND DISCUSSION QUESTIONS

1. Extended week to complete assignments
2. Formatting and references
3. Submission of assignments on Blackboard
4. Participation in class discussions

Additional Resources for Online Discussions

Communication and Feedback

5. *Students are expected to:*
6. *The professor is expected to:*
7. Please post questions in forum "Questions about moving to the online environment, deadlines, class expectations etc."
8. Don't be connected to class 24–7
9. Keep connected through GroupMe
10. Office Hours

A final note in this document said, "Most importantly, let's be patient and understanding with one another! Neither of us signed up for an online class, but that's what we've got."

This document shows clarification of tasks and expectations, clear directions, and a commitment to assisting students as they moved to the online environment at a very stressful time for everyone. The document also showed care for the students' well-being as they adapted to a new way of attending classes. For seven of the 12 students, this was the first time they were taking what then was going to be a full online class, so adaptations and understanding from the part of everyone was paramount.

Another important aspect was the provision of timely, relevant, specific, and formative feedback. Luciana provided online feedback individually and to groups and shared rubrics for each assignment so students knew exactly how they were going to be graded. The rubrics for each assignment were shared the same day an assignment was posted to Blackboard, and students were asked to review the assignment sheet along with the rubric and ask questions to clarify anything they did not understand. Feedback was provided in written, audio, and video forms so students had access to multiple forms of feedback, which is a critical part of online teaching and learning (Olesova & de Oliveira, 2015).

Domain 4: Assessment and Evaluation

For Domain 4, *assessment of learning* and *performance and evaluation of instructional effectiveness* were identified as competencies. Some examples for these competencies were communication of assessment criteria with specific design of engaging assessments for the course and provision of information to students about their progress. Key assessments included a lesson plan that students developed on their own as part of learning how to plan content area instruction for MLs. It followed a specific lesson plan template that Luciana has developed and implemented over the past 15 years of work with pre-service and in-service teachers (See de Oliveira, 2020, for information on planning using the lesson plan template). Students exchanged lesson plans and provided peer feedback on each other's plans and also submitted a draft to the instructor for formative feedback. Students then incorporated the feedback received by peers and the instructor before turning in a final draft.

Closely monitoring student performance is very important in online courses, in general, and especially important during a pandemic. Luciana not only assessed students formatively to ensure they were making progress but also discussed progress with them and adjusted assignment due dates and expectations as needed. Students assisted in the process of evaluation of instructional materials and suggested modifications which were made based on student feedback.

Domain 5: Management

This domain includes the following competencies: *management of an environment that fosters learning and performance* and *management of the instructional process through the appropriate use of technology*. In terms of *management of an environment that fosters learning and performance*, it is important for instructors to anticipate situations that may affect learning. Luciana used specific strategies for this by chunking content into manageable parts and developing lessons in a logical sequence. Each week had clear and distinguishable content marked on the syllabus and adapted as necessary as students provided feedback on the class, explained under Domain 4. Establishment of expectations was one of the most important pieces of this course. The variety of means for course communication helped create a community among online students. Luciana was particularly concerned about building social presence as they moved to the online environment as she knew this is a critical component of teaching online successfully (Richardson & Swan, 2003).

For *management of the instructional process through the appropriate use of technology*, selection of appropriate technology tools for instruction and assessment is seen as a critical component of a successful online course (Major, 2015; Olesova & de Oliveira, 2016). Luciana used Blackboard as a learning management system to design and deliver the course. Because she was already familiar with this LMS and had used it several times to teach online at a previous institution, she was able to use it without much effort or learning

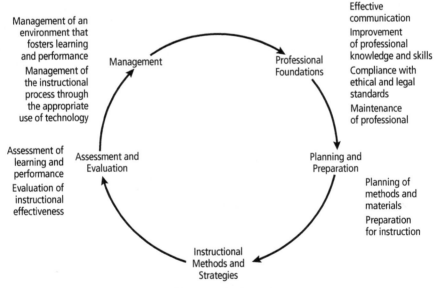

Figure 1.1 Competencies in teaching an ESOL methods course.

involved. She used most of the features available and was able to provide students with experiential learning tools such as audio and video materials that they had to listen to and watch in order to learn more about teaching ESOL students. These were all important components of the course that also kept students engaged and interested in the course content.

CONCLUSION

This self-study showed how specific instructor competencies were expressed based on adaptations made to a face-to-face ESOL Methods course that was moved to the online environment as a result of the COVID-19 pandemic. We provided examples of practice to show how required skills, attitudes, and knowledge of a competent instructor were used in five domains to provide best practices and explained how these constitute model practices for online teaching and learning.

Our findings confirmed that effective instructional strategies in alignment with instructor competences to move from face-to-face teaching environments to online can help facilitate an engaging and interactive online community of learners. Facilitating engagement and interaction is one of the most important skills in online teaching where instructor and students are separated in terms of space or time. Instructor's technological skills are also very important because instructors are able to provide diverse ways of learning, i.e., in addition to traditional text-based feedback, audio and video feedback can be provided.

REFERENCES

Albanese, M. A., Mejicano, G., Mullan, P., Kokotailo, P., & Gruppen, L. (2008). Defining characteristics of educational competencies. *Medical Education, 42*(3), 248–255. https://doi.org/10.1111/j.1365-2923.2007.02996.x

Ball, D., & Forzani, F. (2010). Teaching skillful teaching. *Educational Leadership, 68*(4), 40–45. http://www.ascd.org/publications/educational-leadership/dec10/vol68/num04/Teaching-Skillful-Teaching.aspx

Carraccio, C., Wolfsthal, S. D., Englander, R., Ferentz, K., & Martin, C. (2002). Shifting paradigms: From Flexner to competencies. *Academic Medicine, 77*(5), 361–367. https://doi.org/10.1097/00001888-200205000-00003

Cavanaugh, J. (2005). Teaching online—A time comparison. *Online Journal of Distance Learning Administration, 8*(1). https://www.westga.edu/~distance/ojdla/spring81/cavanaugh81.htm

Cochran-Smith, M., & Lytle, S. L. (2004). Practitioner inquiry, knowledge, and university culture. In J. Loughran, M. L. Hamilton, V. LaBoskey, & T. Russell (Eds.), *International handbook of research of self-study of teaching and teacher education practices* (pp. 602–649). Kluwer.

Corbin, J., & Strauss, A. (2014). *Basics of qualitative research: Techniques and procedures for developing grounded theory*. SAGE.

Crawford-Ferre, H. G., & Wiest, L. R. (2012). Effective online instruction in higher education. *Quarterly Review of Distance Education, 13*(1), 11–14.

Creasman, P. A. (2014). *Considerations in online course design* (IDEA paper #52). The IDEA Center. https://www.ideaedu.org/idea_papers/considerations-in-online-course-design/

Creswell, J. (2009). *Research design: Qualitative, quantitative, and mixed methods approaches*. SAGE.

de Oliveira, L. C. (2020). Planning and application using a language-based approach to content instruction (LACI) in multilingual classrooms. *MinneTESOL Journal, 36*(2), 1–8. https://minnetesoljournal.org/category/journal-archive/mtj-2020-2/

Dinkelman, T. (2003). Self-study in teacher education: A means and ends tool for promoting reflective teaching. *Journal of Teacher Education, 54*, 6–18. https://doi.org/10.1177/0022487102238654

Field, H. (1979). Competency based teacher education (CBTE): A review of the literature. *British Journal of In-Service Education, 6*(1), 39–42. https://doi.org/10.1080/0305763790060109

Fish, W. W., & Wickersham, L. E. (2009). Best practices for online instructors: Reminders. *Quarterly Review of Distance Education, 10*(3), 279–284.

Fletcher, T., & Bullock, S. M. (2012). Enacting literacy pedagogies: A collaborative self-study between teacher educators in physical education and science. *Studying Teacher Education: A Journal of Self-Study of Teacher Education Practices, 8*(1), 19–33. https://doi.org/10.1080/17425964.2012.657011

Grabowski, B. L., Beaudoin, M., & Koszalka, T. A. (2016). Competencies for designers, instructors, and online learners. In N. Rushby & D. Surry (Eds.), *Wiley handbook of learning technology* (pp. 221–241). Wiley.

Hamilton, M. L., & Pinnegar, S. (1998). The value and promise of self-study. In M. L. Hamilton (Ed.), *Reconceptualizing teaching practice: Self-study in teacher education* (pp. 235–246). Falmer Press.

Hodges, C., Moore, S., Lockee, B., Trust, T., & Bond, A. (2020, March 27). The difference between emergency remote teaching and online teaching. *EDUCAUSE*. https://er.educause.edu/articles/2020/3/the-difference-between-emergency-remote-teaching-and-online-learning

Klein, J., Spector, J. M., Grabowski, B. L., & de la Teja, I. (2004). *Instructor competencies: Standards for face-to-face, online, and blended settings* (3rd ed.). Information Age Publishing.

Loughran, J. (2005). Researching teaching about teaching: Self-study of teacher education practices. *Studying Teacher Education, 1*(1), 5–16. https://doi.org/10.1080/17425960500039777

Loughran, J. (2007). Researching teacher education practices: Responding to the challenges, demands, and expectations of self-study. *Journal of Teacher Education, 58*(1), 12–20. https://doi.org/10.1177/0022487106296217

Major, C. H. (2015). *Teaching online: A guide to theory, research, and practice*. Johns Hopkins University Press.

Martin, F., Budhrani, K., Kumar, S., & Ritzhaupt, A. (2019). Award-winning faculty online teaching practices: Roles and competencies. *Online Learning, 23*(1), 184–205. https://doi.org/10.24059/olj.v23i1.1329

Martin, F., Budhrani, K., & Wang, C. (2019). Examining faculty perception of their readiness to teach online. *Online Learning, 23*(3), 97–119. https://doi.org/10.24059/olj.v23i3.1555

Nilsson, P., & Loughran, J. (2012). Developing and accessing professional knowledge as a science teacher educator: Learning about teaching from student teachers. In S. Bullock & T. Russell (Eds.), *Self-studies of science teacher education practices* (pp. 121–138). Springer.

O'Flaherty, J., & Beal, E. M. (2018). Core competencies and high leverage practices of the beginning teacher: A synthesis of the literature. *Journal of Education for Teaching, 44*(4), 461–478. https://doi.org/10.1080/02607476.2018.1450826

Olesova, L., & de Oliveira, L. C. (2015). Using embedded audio feedback for formative assessment purposes in teaching about English language learners. In S. Koc, P. Wachira, & X. Liu, (Eds.), *Assessment in online and blended learning environments* (pp. 125–142). Information Age Publishing.

Olesova, L., & de Oliveira, L. C. (2016). Teaching technology to ELLs. In N. Li (Ed.), *Teaching ELLs across content areas: Issues and strategies* (pp. 157–185). Information Age Publishing.

Olesova, L., & de Oliveira, L. (2017). Using feedback in ESL and EFL asynchronous online environments. In J. Perren, K. Kelch, J. Byun, S. Cervantes, & S. Safavi (Eds.), *Application of CALL theory in ESL and EFL environments* (pp. 206–222). IGI Global.

Pinnegar, S. (1998). Methodological perspectives: Introduction. In M. L. Hamilton (Ed.), *Reconceptualizing teaching practice: Self-study in teacher education* (pp. 31–33). Falmer.

Pinnegar, S., & Hamilton, M. L. (2009). *Self-study of practice as a genre of qualitative research*. Springer.

Richardson, J., & Swan, K. (2003). An examination of social presence in online courses in relation to students' perceived learning and satisfaction. *Journal of Asynchronous Learning Network, 7*(1), 68–88. https://doi.org/10.24059/olj.v7i1.1864

Shulman, L. (1987). Knowledge and teaching: Foundations of the new reform. *Harvard Educational Review, 57*(1), 1–23.

Thomas, J. E., & Graham, C. R. (2019). Online teaching competencies in observational rubrics: What are institutions evaluating? *Distance Education, 40*(1), 114–132. https://doi.org/10.1080/01587919.2018.1553564

Vanassche, E., & Kelchtermans, G. (2015) The state of the art in self-study of teacher education practices: A systematic literature review. *Journal of Curriculum Studies, 47*(4), 508–528. https://doi.org/10.1080/00220272.2014.995712

Wang, Y., Wang., Y., Stein, D., Liu, Q., & Chen, W. (2021). The structure of Chinese beginning online instructors' competencies: Evidence from Bayesian factor analysis. *Journal of Computers in Education, 8*, 411–440. https://doi.org/10.1007/s40692-021-00186-9

Zou, B., Huang, L., Ma, W., & Qiu, Y. (2021). Evaluation of the effectiveness of EFL online teaching during the COVID-19 pandemic. *SAGE Open, 1*(4). https://doi.org/10.1177/21582440211054491

CHAPTER 2

HOW EMERGENCY REMOTE ONLINE LANGUAGE TEACHING INFORMED POST-LOCKDOWN LANGUAGE TEACHING PRACTICES

The Case of Two Chinese EFL Elementary Teachers

Carla Meskill
State University of New York

Dongni Guo
State University of New York

Fang Wang
State University of New York

Wuri Kusumastuti
State University of New York

Pedagogies for Equitable Access, pages 17–38
Copyright © 2024 by Information Age Publishing
www.infoagepub.com
All rights of reproduction in any form reserved.

ABSTRACT

This longitudinal case study explores the experiences of two elementary English as a foreign language (EFL) teachers in China during the pandemic-induced shift to online instruction. The study, spanning from the lockdown period to the return to regular classrooms, relies on semi-structured interviews, course artifacts, and archived class recordings. The teachers leveraged online teaching for increased interactivity, leading to the adoption of new practices post-lockdown. The analysis reveals three major areas of technology-induced change: (a) tailoring instruction; (b) managing instruction; and (c) extending instruction. The study emphasizes the positive impact of emergency remote online language teaching (EROLT) on teacher professional development, highlighting the importance of direct experience with instructional technologies in teacher education.

The COVID-19 outbreak in China disrupted K–12 education. To counter this, China initiated fully online teaching. For 3 months, online instruction became the norm for English language teachers. Teachers' cognition (Gao & Zhang, 2020), teaching strategies (Zsohar & Smith, 2008), and emotions (Naylor & Nyanjom, 2021) concerning their work were significantly impacted by both the rapid shift to online instruction and the return to the regular classroom.

Teaching languages online is challenging under the best of circumstances (Meskill et al., 2022). In China, however, government-supplied digital resources and technical assistance provided some support (Zhou et al., 2020). Resources in the form of video recorded models of exemplary online teaching, mini lessons, supporting applications, and tools were rapidly developed and made accessible to educators. The Chinese government developed and distributed an elementary school network cloud of online courses recorded by expert teachers (Ministry of Education of the People's Republic of China, 2020). Further, teachers across the country quickly developed and shared with one another their own materials and approaches via social networking. They learned strategies for online teaching, changed and/or incorporated their prior teaching practices, and encouraged their students to learn on screen without on-site supervision (Zhou, 2020). Teachers also helped their students adapt to online learning environments and their tools (Gao & Zhang, 2020). In this way, teachers experienced a great deal of growth and success and quickly progressed from being lost and anxious to gradually adapting and being creative (Zhou, 2020).

This qualitative case study tracked two Chinese elementary English educators who swiftly shifted to online teaching for three months and then resumed in-person classes. Our focus was on the strategies they used to enhance interaction among themselves, students, and parents. We aimed to understand the influence of these online interactions on their post-lockdown teaching practices. As such, our overarching research question was how EFL teachers' experiences with the affordances and efficiencies of online instruction informed their during-lockdown and post-lockdown practices.

PERSPECTIVES

Research on online instruction suggests that interactivity, particularly student-teacher interactivity, plays a critical role when it comes to student satisfaction, retention, and overall learning experiences (Kuo et al., 2013; Mahle, 2011; Walker & Koralesky, 2021). In addition to influencing academic achievement, research also suggests that peer interactions positively impact learning (Clinton & Wilson, 2019; Tare et al., 2014). During the pandemic, emergency remote online language teaching (EROLT) brought new emphasis on the importance of peer interactions as part of learning (Wong, 2020) and the need for opportunities for students to interact when learning online (Bond, 2020). It has also been observed that when learning online, students, especially younger students, can gain a sense of comfort and belonging through interactions with others. Choi and Chung (2021), for example, emphasized the importance of specifically encouraging EFL learners to participate and thereby experience a sense of community.

In the field of language education, it is widely accepted that active, purposeful interactions in the target language are central to its acquisition (Loewen & Sato, 2018; Mackey, 1999; Savignon, 1987, 1991; Spada & Lightbown, 2009; Swain, 2006). Online contexts are particularly well suited for such interactions—both synchronous and asynchronous—and taxonomies of online language learning affordances tend to ascribe preeminence to this dimension (Meskill & Anthony, 2014, 2015; Thorne et al., 2009). For this study, we viewed online pedagogical actions and interactions as social processes that could lead to positive language learning experiences. Thus, this inquiry considers the various forms of online interaction that language educators capitalized on during EROLT and if and how such online forms of interactivity accrued value such that these practices carried over into the post-lockdown classroom.

LITERATURE REVIEW

Online language education has been actively practiced and researched since the early 1990s. Multiple affordances of the online environment lend themselves perfectly to the goals and processes of contemporary second and foreign language instruction and acquisition (Meskill & Anthony, 2015). Indeed, for language education, the affordances of both synchronous and asynchronous interactivity with accompanying visual and aural media are reported to greatly augment teaching and learning experiences, rendering the online platform in some ways superior to the face-to-face language classroom (Meskill et al., 2020, 2022). Studies have determined that teaching languages online transcends time and space limitations in addition to making learning more fun, motivating, and interactive (e.g., Demouy et al., 2016; Gao & Zhang, 2020). In addition, Zhou (2020) discusses four advantages of online teaching: (a) a sense of safety for teachers and students; (b) equity of access to educational resources; (c) timely communication, feedback, and management; and (d) student engagement.

Despite such advantages, online language teaching may prove complicated and challenging for some novice teachers who lack online teaching experience (De Paepe et al., 2018). During the lockdown, for example, Putri (2021) found that EFL teachers were challenged when trying to provide feedback to learners and when teaching productive skills like speaking and writing. In China, Zhou (2020) identified three challenges for online language teaching: the choice of teaching platform(s), student self-management supervision, and teacher anxiety. Zhou (2020) also reports teacher helplessness, sadness, and depression due to insufficient support for dealing with such unfamiliar teaching environments but that teachers gradually adapted to the online format through developing new ways of teaching. Gradual adaptation was also a prominent outcome of a recent study on language teacher preparation for rural education in Asia (Meskill, Kusumastuti, Guo, & Wang, 2023).

Early research on online language teaching during the lockdown mainly focused on the challenges and difficulties of online language teaching (e.g., Putri, 2021), and teaching modalities (e.g., Jiang et al., 2020) with most studies dealing with higher education (e.g., Huang et al., 2020). In more recent studies, there has been a focus on teachers' resilience and ingenuity (e.g., Meskill, Kusumastuti, & Guo, 2023; Meskill, Kusumastuti, Guo, Wang, & Ramos, 2023). In line with this work, our inquiry focuses on the learning experiences of elementary EFL educators who made the three-month emergency transition to online language teaching and then back to their regular classrooms with the goal of determining what they learned and how it impacted their post-lockdown teaching.

METHODS

Our research question focused on how EFL teachers' experiences with the affordances and efficiencies of online instruction informed their during-lockdown and post-lockdown practices. Using a case study design, we explored the experiences of two Chinese EFL teachers in making the emergency transition to online teaching, adapting their practices accordingly, and returning to their regular classrooms after the 3-month lockdown. The two teachers engaged with us in ongoing semi-structured interviews over the course of one year. A case study design was deemed to be appropriate to gain in-depth understanding of subjects' experiences and their thoughts about them (Yafaei & Rais, 2019). Given that our aim was to go deeply into the experiences of two Chinese EFL teachers as opposed to generalization, the case study design was appropriate for the exploration of such contextualized phenomena (Hatch, 2002).

Context

The elementary schools where our two focal teachers taught were similar to most elementary schools found in large and medium-sized cities in China (one taught in a small city and the other in the capital of Hunan Province). Class sizes in such schools tend to be 50 students, most of whom come from middle-class families. During the pandemic, the Chinese government supplied all language educators with videoclips of model online language lessons, online language teaching resources, and technical assistance.

Participants

Two subjects were recruited to participate in the study. We posted recruitment information with a consent form on an online alumni group from First Normal University in China. One EFL teacher replied and was willing to participate in the study. Another subject was recommended by a colleague and agreed to participate. Each qualified as they were elementary public school EFL teachers who had temporarily moved their classes fully online during the lockdown. The two participants are referred to by their pseudonyms: Yu and Li. Table 2.1 provides an overview of their backgrounds.

As shown in Table 2.1, the two informants were elementary public school EFL teachers. Yu taught English for 5 years. For the first four of these years, she worked for a private language school as an online English teacher. In 2019 she began teaching English to third grade students (Beginning level) at an urban public elementary school. Li earned her bachelor's degree in English education in 2011. She taught EFL in urban elementary public schools for ten years. During the lockdown, she taught fifth-grade students.

TABLE 2.1 Subject Demographics					
Name	Gender	Age	Educational degree	Teaching grade	Years of teaching
Yu	Female	23	Bachelor of Arts in English Education	Grade 3	5
Li	Female	31	Bachelor of Arts in English Education	Grade 5	10

Data Collection

Data were collected via WeChat interviews. Each participant was interviewed a minimum of three times with each interview lasting from 30 to 60 minutes. Interviewees were first asked to discuss their prior teaching experiences and their shifts in teaching strategies due to the lockdown. In the final interview, each discussed new strategies they used once they had gone back to in-person teaching, and how online teaching experiences during the lockdown informed these post-lockdown practices. All interviews were conducted in Chinese and audio-recorded using freely available sound recorder apps. The two authors who wrote and spoke both Chinese and English conducted the interviews and translated the transcripts. They individually translated the Chinese manuscripts into English and then discussed discrepancies between the translations until the rate of agreement about the interview transcriptions reached eighty percent.

Data Analysis

Through iterative processes of reading, discussing, coding, interpreting, aligning, and revising and after multiple rounds of transcript analysis the authors collectively identified three major themes that addressed our research question: managing instruction, tailoring instruction, and expanding interactions. These we illustrate and discuss in detail in the Findings section.

Positionality

The lead author and head of the research team examines how digital screens are used in classrooms, online instruction, and educator professional development. The other authors are doctoral students who share interest in online language education. Drawing from our collective experiences as language educators, we bring specific perspectives to the research. Guo and Wang (native Chinese) focus on language teacher's pedagogical development to promote effective teacher-student-parent interactions. Kusumastuti explores online language learning communities and autonomous learning practices with technologies. Due to such experiences and research interests, along with a shared view of language acquisition as a socially complex phenomenon, the team has investigated the responses of language teaching professionals around the world as they transitioned to online teaching under emergency circumstances. For this current study, we integrated our expertise to examine specific cases of Chinese EFL teachers.

FINDINGS

Before their three-month lockdown, Yu and Li reported that teaching and learning interactions in their classrooms had been mostly limited to teacher-fronted classroom lectures. Logistics such as large class sizes and curricular/assessment emphasis prohibited them from including various forms of interactivity, strategies that became central and valued during the lockdown. They reported that the interactivity among students, teachers and students, and parents and their children and teachers that was made possible online brought new and positive pedagogical practices they had not formerly explored. When instruction moved online, they found that online forms of interaction represented opportunities to manage, tailor and extend instructional activity in highly positive and productive ways. When Li and Yu returned to the live classroom, they continued to capitalize on their online teaching experiences.

As illustrated in Figure 2.1, we identified three areas of growth that can be defined in the following ways:

Managing instruction: Student progress tracking tools, automated grading, online grading tools, performance reports with teacher comments, and digital materials integration tools.
Tailoring instruction: Online communication tools to facilitate conversations with individuals and groups of students based on need, tailored assignments and quizzes, tracking individual learner progress.
Extending instruction: Affordances supporting communication such as notifications, shared contacts, liking/responding, tracking/following, rewards (badges, emojis, gifts), and connecting and coordinating with students and their parents.

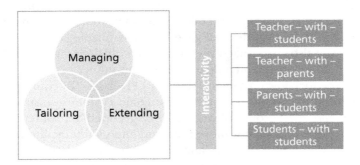

Figure 2.1 Shifts in interactivity.

These efficiencies in tailoring, managing, and extending instruction freed up both teachers to do more teaching and less classroom management. Further, the fact that students could monitor their own learning online along with automated administrative reminders and notifications saved time.

Tailoring Instruction

Both Li and Yu reported that, unlike in pre-lockdown, teacher-fronted classrooms, in online forums they could easily and efficiently tailor their instruction to specific learning needs. They cited the efficiencies afforded by online tools as directly promoting and supporting interactivity.

Teacher–Student

Before the lockdown, when Li found that students had difficulty with what she taught, she had to find additional time in her class to re-teach that concept. During the lockdown, however, she recorded mini lessons so that students could watch them on their own, stopping, reviewing, and restarting the videos as their learning needs dictated. Based on the success of this approach, after the lockdown Li continued to record and upload micro lesson videos (5–10 minutes) for her students to refer to when they had trouble. At the same time, she gave students corresponding online exercises. She reported:

> Not using class time for reviewing unmastered concepts offers two advantages: better teaching efficiency and improved student outcomes. Limited class time hindered repetitive explanations, but micro lesson videos let students review until confident. This approach pleases students and parents. (Li)

As evidenced in the interview excerpt above, Li used instructional strategies proactively to meet students' needs and to individualize their language learning. By doing so, closer relationships with students developed; she got to know individual learners and determine what would best support their learning. While she provided self-paced, freely available language learning resources, she also encouraged students to identify their own learning challenges and to seek help and guidance from her online.

Before the lockdown, Yu lectured to her EFL classes. By contrast, during the lockdown, she found that online she could customize instruction for individual and small groups of students. She grouped her students according to their levels and spent more time and energy interacting with them at their current level of English language learning. Further, to help struggling students understand the government supplied expert EFL teaching videos that she assigned, she grouped students online to review the videos together while she assisted them via clarification questions. She found her students highly engaged in such online activity.

Yu also tailored her instruction by establishing similar level study groups. In these groups, teachers and students focused on the same learning materials (e.g., government supplied expert EFL teaching videos, content clips), and discussed and practiced the new language modeled with one another. She reported that in these small groups, students were more engaged and confident in their learning.

With 50 students, Yu also found these practices time-consuming. After the lockdown, therefore, she switched to conducting tailored sessions asynchronously via Q&A. She also, like Li, pre-recorded mini-teaching videos to assign to struggling students in response to their specific needs.

Through their EROLT experiences, both Li and Yu found that they could assist individual and small groups of students with similar needs. They did so by providing online tailored learning opportunities in the form of (a) posting mini-teaching videos; (b) interacting with students asynchronously around recorded teaching segments; and (c) assigning online exercises as review and remediation. These technology-based tailoring strategies were so successful that they carried over into post-lockdown classrooms.

Students–Parents

Prior to the lockdown, parents' roles had been limited to monitoring whether their children completed their homework. During the lockdown Yu found that parents could be called on to assist her and that they were invaluable instructional assets. She often assigned parents to partner with their children to complete assignments. For example, students collaborated with their parents to script, record, and stream homemade videos for other students to learn from. After the lockdown, Yu continued to encourage her students and their parents to make English videos at home.

> I asked my students to finish English conversation tasks with their parents at home and to record the process as videos or audios. They shared and submitted their digital products to social networks (WeChat Group) or Learner Management System (e.g., Yiqizuoye). I found parents and students created so much excellent work that I used them in my live classes. Also, when I reviewed their video work, I found students were more excited and relaxed in such a family environment. For me, I saved a lot of time and energy on the teaching process, and I was able to spend more time preparing and designing better lessons. (Yu)

In our interviews Yu concluded that supportive and collaborative relationships between students and parents were essential during EROLT.

Managing Instruction

As a result of their EROLT experiences, both teachers learned that they could manage their students' learning more effectively and efficiently using online tools. Tracking student progress and responding to their needs became something they both continued to do when they returned to the regular classroom. They both reported that these management efficiencies impacted interactions in many productive ways.

Teacher–Student

Li found that constantly asking questions during synchronous sessions was a good way for her to interact with her students. This strategy helped her compensate for the limitations of not seeing students' facial expressions as most turned off their cameras. By asking questions, she could tell whether students were understanding. The strategy also ensured that students were concentrating. She observed:

> Students, being young, can easily get distracted by activities like eating, playing, and watching unrelated things. Hence, frequent questioning keeps them attentive, ensuring they listen; otherwise, they can't answer. The second aim is to gauge their comprehension of our lessons. (Li)

Interactivity between teacher and students around online digital homework also brought opportunities to manage student learning more efficiently. For instance, before the lockdown, Li assigned homework on paper and students would not see her evaluation or comments until these were handed back the next day or beyond. During the lockdown Li used the app *Yingyubao* to assign digital homework and students thereby received immediate feedback on their work. She observed positive responses from students in this respect:

> I found that the number of students in the class using the app Yingyubao has been increasing after the lockdown. (Li)

Managing instruction also includes emotional support which further impacts students' learning. During the lockdown Li praised students more and criticized them less than she did prior to the lockdown. She reported focusing more on students' strengths rather than mistakes they might make. She posted positive comments and words of encouragement online to individuals and groups of students. She reported:

> Before the lockdown, students were captive in the classroom despite criticism. During lockdown, I increased praise and reduced criticism to prevent dis-

tancing. This boosted motivation and alignment. Post-lockdown, I prioritize Seewo app for encouragement, not critique, to enhance motivation. (Li)

Based on her experiences with teaching online during the lockdown, she saw that managing instruction and its forms of interaction changed. Li reported that these changes, realizable via technology, were conducive to strengthening teacher-student interaction both academically and emotionally, which consequently improved learning.

Yu found that her young students often felt challenged by their isolation while learning at home on the computer, so she devised a system of rewarding points as a means of improving attention and morale. Children could use their accumulated points to order school supplies, toys, and books that were mailed to their homes. They also earned points to use on digital badges. She continued this practice of offering rewards post-lockdown:

These rewards motivated them a lot. Can you imagine how happy they are when they received gifts! (Yu)

Yu also found that she could video record everyday managerial information and thus have more time and energy for in-class instructional interactions. Further, before the lockdown, Yu used concrete manipulatives to motivate and support learning activities. During the lockdown, she integrated digital games and learning resources in her online classes.

Both Li and Yu made use of online tools to manage instruction, engage students in instructional conversations with, through and around what was jointly viewed on screens (e.g., discussion questions, students' homework), and make their learning experiences more productive. These positive and constructive screen-mediated interactions not only ensured the continuity of teaching under extraordinary circumstances, but also carried over once instruction returned to the regular classroom.

Parent–Student

Before the lockdown, parents rarely participated in Yu's EFL classes. During the lockdown, Yu encouraged parents to attend online classes with their children to serve as supervisors, facilitators and learning partners. She also directed students to practice English dialogs with their parents:

It was hard for young learners to focus on learning English online. Without parent's supervision, they might be easily attracted by delicious foods, pets or any noises outside and forget to take notes. I also left time for my students to practice English conversations with their parents in online classes. (Yu)

Further, Yu encouraged her students to physically simulate English digital games at home with their parents. For example, Yu asked her students

Figure 2.2 Screenshot from video of parents and child playing color blending game.

to play a color blending game with their parents while explaining the color blending process in English to their parents using the phrase "if you mix... (yellow) with... (blue), you will get... (green)" or by simply using the phrase "This is... (yellow)."

As illustrated in Figure 2.2, Yu orchestrated interactive spaces and opportunities for students and parents to engage in practicing English. This way students had opportunities to experience authentic language in use.

Extending Interactions

Extending interactions refers to communication between students, teachers, and parents beyond the traditional classroom schedule via messaging and social media. This kind of communication became part of online learning activities during the lockdown and, having experienced the power and value of these beyond-the-classroom online communications, both teachers continued with this practice post-lockdown. Indeed, both pointed to this extending of interactions beyond the classroom as pedagogically powerful.

Teacher–Student

Before the lockdown, Yu carried out her courses in person and used few, if any, digital instructional applications. Instead, she prepared paper-based assignments (e.g., reading and writing quizzes) which students finished independently at home. When she shifted her courses online, the period for each class was reduced from 40 minutes to 20 minutes, and she had to make changes. She responded to the move online by using both synchronous and asynchronous online resources and communicative tools with her students. She employed multimodal digital platforms such as *Voov Meeting*, *Yingyubao*, and *Yiqizuoye* to address different language skills. She also used group features to orchestrate interactive synchronous learning activities. In addition, she created pre-recorded videos and uploaded them to Yingyubao. This strategy allowed students to access lessons anytime and to repeat and pause when needed. She also used both synchronous and asynchronous approaches to assign homework and assignments. Formats for assignments included self-test quizzes, dubbing tasks, reading digital picture books, recording English videos, and other creative task-oriented activities.

When Yu returned to in-person classes, she continued to employ these digital resources and applications to extend interactions beyond the classroom. Her post-lockdown classes are now very much blended. She makes the most of online teaching resources to assign homework and quizzes to keep students engaged.

Student–Student

Peer interaction in Li's classes extended from strictly in-class to out-of-class through technology. Before the lockdown, interactions among students were limited to brief role-plays or small group discussions. During lockdown, she created WeChat groups where four or five students could get together and discuss what they were learning, their homework, and so on. She assigned a student leader for each WeChat group who was responsible for gathering questions from group members and reporting them to the teacher. Li would then respond in the specific WeChat group or to the whole class. Li would also assess each group's collaborative work and praise groups that performed well. She reported:

> With over 200 students... This method's efficient as I gather info from leaders, giving quick feedback to multiple students, saving time. Also, small WeChat groups foster mutual trust, combating lockdown loneliness. (Li)

After lockdown, Li continued to group students online. That way students could not only undertake learning activities together during class time, but they could also stay in touch and confer after class. Li could thereby extend interactions beyond the classroom with the help of technology. She reported:

> Lockdown showed group post-class study boosts learning. After, I'll group students for collaborative tasks using the Seewo App's "class housekeeper." They'll collaborate in and out of class. App-based grading and parent access add convenience. I value this app feature over WeChat. (Li)

Interactivity between peers mediated by technology during the lockdown made both teachers aware of the benefits of student interactions during and after class. Through these interactive technologies, students could get support and feedback from their peers with informal peer pressure propelling them to be active learners. The two teachers reported that in their post lockdown classrooms they actively sought more digital tools to help them orchestrate interactivity between students beyond class time.

Teacher–Parent

Before the lockdown, Li's expectations concerning parental involvement were limited to having them check to see if homework got completed on time. During the 3-month lockdown, Li realized that she needed parents' cooperation. Their support helped considerably in terms of both emotional and academic engagement. She began to interact with parents regularly by providing them with details of their children's progress and guiding them to work with their children:

> Online teaching depends on parents' help. During lockdowns, students struggled with focus and mood. Parents are key to maintaining focus, ensuring study, and support. WeChat updates on classes and homework involve parents. If a student seems uninterested, parents asking gently helps conversation. (Li)

Li consequently became aware of the importance of parents in her EFL teaching. She continued these practices after the lockdown by communicating with parents and encouraging their participation in their children's English learning. She also shared students' performance information and guided parents to make use of this:

> Apart from the WeChat, the Seewo app helps parents know their kids' daily performance through my evaluation and grades. As such, when the parents urge or guide their children to study, they know what to start from and how to do it. (Li)

Parent–Student

During the lockdown, Li counted on parents to help regulate students' emotions, urge students to watch assigned videos, and to help with assignments. After the lockdown parents continued to receive online information about their children's learning along with instructions for how to work with their children. Li reported:

> After the epidemic, I create and share short lessons on the Seewo app, highlighting lesson challenges and key points. This helps parents guide their children's learning and fosters better academic interaction between them. (Li)

Before the lockdown, Yu's interactions with her students after class were limited to paper-based homework, which she assigned and later reviewed. During the lockdown, she not only encouraged her students and their parents to complete homework assignments together (e.g., English conversations and interactive games) but also to video record these interactions. Parents uploaded these videos so that Yu could view, comment on, and even share them on her social networks. She also downloaded and shared these videos. In online social media groups, she trained parents how to facilitate their children's learning via videos where she modeled parent-student interactions.

> I made a series of micro courses (around 20 minutes each). In these videos, I invited a little girl as my teaching assistant. She pretended to be my daughter. We learn English together by dancing, singing, playing games, and so on. By doing so, I wanted to show parents how to interact with their kids. They could model the process at home. (Yu)

After the lockdown, Yu and her students' parents continued to engage in online communication in support of English language learning. Her school's administration also realized that parents were eager to communicate with their children's teachers so she facilitated a formal online communication system to maintain this extended interaction.

> On the first day of school after the lockdown, I asked parents to download the app and register, so parents would know their kid's real-time performances at school, such as their grades, class performances. I can also make announcements to them and know whether parents read my messages. (Yu)

For these teachers, instructionally positive forms of interactivity evolved out of their three-month move to online instruction. During the lockdown, they found that technology tools could be used to enhance tailoring, managing and extending learning interactions between and among teachers, students and their parents. Once back in the classroom, they continued to capitalize on these technology features having learned firsthand that using these tools could lead to (a) strengthened communication; (b) increased learning collaborations; (c) closely tailored remediation; and (d) afforded immediate feedback from online learning apps, the teacher and parents. As represented in Figure 2.3, compared to limited interactions before the

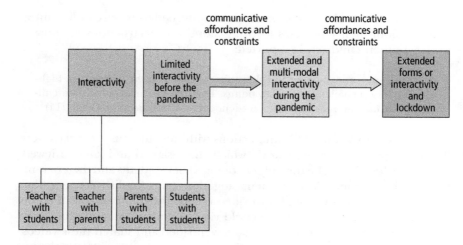

Figure 2.3 Shifts in interactivity.

lockdown, interactions between and among these teachers, their students and their students' parents augmented.

DISCUSSION

Contrary to earlier studies examining EROLT's impact on EFL teachers, our findings indicate that rather than just duplicating their regular classroom practices when teaching remotely (e.g., Gao & Zhang, 2020; Hazaea et al., 2021), these two teachers adapted their teaching to make optimal pedagogical use of technology features to enhance, not replace, their instruction. These technology-supported practices in turn inspired enhanced post-lockdown practices, especially regarding the quality and frequency of teacher-orchestrated interactions with and between students and their parents. In both cases, the EFL teachers reported important shifts in their practices when it came to tailoring and managing instruction to meet learners' needs and extending these interactions beyond the classroom.

A highly salient aspect of these EROLT-inspired changes in instructional practices was the parental involvement that these two teachers orchestrated. Prior to the lockdown, parental involvement in their children's learning was very limited. During the lockdown, parental involvement not only became an important element at that time, but both Li and Yu continued to value and integrate these contributive interactions after returning to their classrooms. This is consistent with the experiences of teachers in other cultural contexts as well (e.g., Budhrani et al., 2021; Sari et al., 2021). Having a supportive adult available to support distance learning students is not a new one, however. On-site adult facilitators for students taking remote classes have been a standard in U.S. high schools for many years. These school personnel sit side-by-side with learners to orient them to online learning, facilitate interactions with the online instructor, develop caring local relationships, and help students to organize and manage their learning (Borup et al., 2019). Additionally, research on parental participation in online high school courses points to the critical roles parents play in "monitoring coursework... encouraging, instructing and organizing" (Borup, 2016, p. 68). In addition to assisting them with management, for Li and Yu parental participation also accomplished direct pedagogical aims: that is, to engage learners in actively practicing the target language. This instructional parental role evolved into an important one that Li and Yu continued to value and encourage by maintaining active online communication channels with students' families in post lockdown instruction.

In terms of interacting with students, both teachers reported an opening up of communication during and beyond class time. Not only could they tailor remedial instruction for learners in need, but they could spend online time, both synchronous and asynchronous, instructing students in creative and targeted ways. Both teachers reported positive reactions to these online modes of interactivity and continued these practices post-lockdown.

Li and Yu also reported finding value in the online student-student interactions they orchestrated during the three-month lockdown. This was an element of language instruction they found difficult, if not impossible, in the regular classroom: guiding students to practice the target language with one another, given large class sizes and limited time. Using online forums, they could assign both in-class and outside-of-class small group work tailored to specific learning needs. Research on both online instruction (Borup et al., 2013) and on online language instruction (Geng & Takatsuka, 2009; Granena, 2016; Ng et al., 2006; Tare et al., 2014; Zeng & Takatsuka, 2009) consistently reports the motivational and instructional value of such peer-to-peer interactivity. Further, the Chinese government had for some time been advocating for more student collaborative work in language classes in their push for communicative language teaching (CLT) approaches (Adamson & Morris, 1997; Hu, 2002; Hu, 2010).

In sum, these teachers' experiences of EROLT brought them new understandings of the extended learning opportunities online teaching represents. These took the form of interacting in new and valuable ways with students and parents. It also brought both teachers to shift from teacher-centered to more student-centered instructional practices afforded by online tools with which they could manage, tailor, and extend instructional interactions. Li and Yu found themselves no longer the sole source of modeling and providing feedback. With so many online resources, their roles shifted to facilitators and mediators who could respond to the needs of small groups and individual students and tailor instruction accordingly. They also reported recognizing the importance of students' well-being and continued to exercise empathy, provide encouragement, and involve parents as instructional/emotional supports. In short, the 3 months that these teachers spent learning to teach language online under emergency circumstances paid off in terms of their mastery of technology-enhanced language pedagogy.

Limitations

This case study design weighted depth over breadth as regards data collection. Data collected were in the form of in-depth, ongoing interviews whereby subjects reported on their practices pre, during and post the three-month lockdown in China. Clearly, more direct observation of instruction would serve to gain additional perspectives and further deepen our understandings about reported shifts in instructional interactions.

CONCLUSION

The goal of this study was to contribute to our growing understanding of K–12 online language teaching and learning. To understand the pre, during, and post-lockdown experiences of two language educators, we undertook an in-depth case study focusing on perceptions and instructional innovations of two elementary EFL teachers who, like all teachers in China, were forced to move their teaching online for three months under emergency conditions. The unique Chinese context, whereby teachers were supported through government-generated videos, workshops, and technical assistance, speaks to the importance of direct and supported experiences with technologies to reshape instructional practice (Becker & Ravitz, 1999; Meskill et al., 2020; Pifarre, 2019). For both Yu and Li, concepts and implementations of language learning interactions shifted them from using instructor-fronted recitations to authentic, engaged interactions in English, a shift that they reported was welcomed by both learners and their parents. Indeed, both educators reported that there was an increased enthusiasm and sense of success among students in learning the language when they orchestrated online forms of instructional interactivity. This suggests that K–12 EFL teachers in general might well benefit from specialized professional development and ongoing technical support while they experiment with different forms of teaching online. In China, this is especially relevant at a time when more communicatively oriented language teaching practices are being advocated.

Online instructional interactions differ markedly from those limited to traditional live classroom settings (Keaton & Gilbert, 2020), especially when it comes to language education (Meskill & Anthony, 2014, 2015). As these two EFL teachers discovered during their country's brief lockdown period, online communication tools can be used in any number of ways to support interactions that augment online language learning experiences in and beyond the classroom.

ACKNOWLEDGMENTS

The authors would like to thank Roberto Ramos for his support and guidance.

REFERENCES

Adamson, B., & Morris, P. (1997). The English curriculum in the People's Republic of China. *Comparative Education Review, 41*(1), 3–26.

Becker, H., & Ravitz, J. (1999). The influence of computer and internet use on teachers' pedagogical practices and perceptions. *Journal of Research on Computing in Education, 31*(4), 356–384. https://doi.org/10.1080/08886504.1999.10782260

Bond, M. (2020). Schools and emergency remote education during the COVID-19 pandemic: A living rapid systematic review. *Asian Journal of Distance Education, 15*(2), 191–247. http://www.asianjde.com/ojs/index.php/AsianJDE/article/view/517

Borup, J. (2016). Teacher perceptions of parent engagement at a cyber high school. *Journal of Research on Technology in Education, 48*(2), 67–83. https://doi.org/10.1080/15391523.2016.1146560

Borup, J., Chambers, C. B., & Stimson, R. (2019). K–12 Student perceptions of online teacher and on-site facilitator support in supplemental online courses. *Online Learning, 23*(4), 253–280. http://doi.org/10.24059/olj.v23i4.1565

Borup, J., Graham, C., & Davies, R. (2013). The nature of adolescent learner interaction in a virtual high school setting: Virtual high school interactions. *Journal of Computer Assisted Learning, 29*(2), 153–167. https://doi.org/10.1111/j.1365-2729.2012.00479.x

Budhrani, K., Martin, F., Malabanan, O., & Espiritu, J. (2021). How did parents balance it all? Work-from-home parents' engagement in academic and support roles during remote learning. *Journal of Online Learning Research, 7*(2), 153–184.

Choi, L., & Chung, S. (2021). Navigating online language teaching in uncertain times: Challenges and strategies of EFL educators in creating a sustainable technology-mediated language learning environment. *Sustainability, 13*(14), 7664. https://doi.org/10.3390/su13147664

Clinton, V., & Wilson, N. (2019). More than chalkboards: Classroom spaces and collaborative learning attitudes. *Learning Environments Research, 22*(3), 325–344. https://doi.org/10.1007/s10984-019-09287-w

Demouy, V., Jones, A., Kan, Q., Kukulska-Hulme, A., & Eardley, A. (2016). Why and how do distance learners use mobile devices for language learning? *The EuroCALL Review, 24*(1), 10–24.

De Paepe, L., Zhu, C., & DePryck, K. (2018). Online language teaching: Teacher perceptions of effective communication tools, required skills and challenges of online teaching. *Journal of Interactive Learning Research, 29*(1). 129–142.

Gao, L. X., & Zhang, L. J. (2020). Teacher learning in difficult times: Examining foreign language teachers' cognitions about online teaching to tide over COVID-19. *Frontiers in Psychology, 11*(549653), 1–14. https://doi.org/10.3389/fpsyg.2020.549653

Geng, Z., & Takatsuka, S. (2009). Task-based peer-peer collaborative dialog in a computer-mediated learning environment in the EFL context. *System, 37*(3), 434–446. https://doi.org/10.1016/j.system.2009.01.003

Granena, G. (2016). Individual versus interactive task-based performance through voice-based computer-mediated communication. *Language Learning & Technology, 20*(3), 40–59.

Hatch, J. A. (2002). *Doing qualitative research in education settings*. State University of New York Press.

Hazaea, A. N., Bin-Hady, W. R. A., & Toujani, M. M. (2021). Emergency remote English language teaching in the Arab league countries: Challenges and remedies. *Computer-Assisted Language Learning Electronic Journal*, 201–222. https://doi.org/10.1016/j.techsoc.2020.101317

Hu, G. (2002). English language teaching in the People's Republic of China. In R. Silver, G. Hu, & M. Lino (Eds.), *English language education in China, Japan, and Singapore* (pp. 1–77). National Institute of Education, Nanyang Technological University.

Hu, W. (2010). Communicative language teaching in the Chinese environment. *US–China Education Review, 7*(6), 78–82. https://files.eric.ed.gov/fulltext/ED511286.pdf

Huang, M., Shi, Y., & Yang, X. (2020). Emergency remote teaching of English as a foreign language during COVID-19: Perspectives from a university in China. *International Journal of Educational Research and Innovation, 15*, 400–418. https://doi.org/10.46661/ijeri.5351

Jiang, H., Jiang, L., & Yu, R. (2020). The construction of an online interactive teaching model during the school postponed of COVID-19 pandemic. *China Education Technology, 399*, 40–41.

Keaton, W., & Gilbert, A. (2020). Successful online learning: What does learner interaction with peers, instructors and parents look like? *Journal of Online Learning Research, 6*(2), 129–154. https://www.learntechlib.org/primary/p/215616/

Kuo, Y. C., Walker, A. E., Belland, B. R., & Schroder, K. E. (2013). A predictive study of student satisfaction in online education programs. *The International Review of Research in Open and Distributed Learning, 14*(1), 16–39. https://doi.org/10.19173/irrodl.v14i1.1338

Loewen, S., & Sato, M. (2018). Interaction and instructed second language acquisition. *Language Teaching, 51*(3), 285–329. https://doi.org/10.1017/S0261444818000125

Mackey, A. (1999). Input, interaction, and second language development: An empirical study of input, interaction, and second language development. *Studies in Second Language Acquisition, 21*(4), 557–588. https://doi.org/10.1017/S0272263199004027

Mahle, M. (2011). Effects of interactivity on student achievement and motivation in distance education. *Quarterly Review of Distance Education, 12*(3), 207–215.

Meskill, C., & Anthony, N. (2014). Synchronous polyvocality in new media/new learning: Online Russian educators' instructional strategies. *System, 42*, 177–188.

Meskill, C., & Anthony, N. (2015). *Teaching languages online*. Multilingual Matters.

Meskill, C., Anthony, N., & Sadykova, G. (2020). Teaching languages online: Professional vision in the making. *Language Learning & Technology, 24*(3), 160–175. http://hdl.handle.net/10125/44745

Meskill, C., Anthony, N., & Sadykova, G. (2022). Learning how to teach languages online: Voices from the field. *Online Learning, 26*(4), 494–518.

Meskill, C., Kusumastuti, W. P, & Guo, D. (2023). From emergency transitions to teaching English online: Three cases. In K. Sadeghi, M. Thomas & F. Ghaderi (Eds.), *Technology-enhanced language teaching and learning: Lessons from the Covid-19 Pandemic* (pp.43–56). Bloomsbury.

Meskill, C., Kusumastuti, W. P., Guo, D., & Wang, F. (2023). Preparing English language teachers for rural education: Pedagogically creative responses to online language teaching in China and Indonesia. In P. C. Iida, E. Mikulec, & M. F. Agnello (Eds.), *English language education in rural contexts: Theory, research, and practices* (pp. 127–144). Brill Sense.

Meskill, C., Kusumastuti, W., Guo, D., Wang, F., & Ramos, R. (2023). Emergency remote EFL instruction in Brazil, China, and Indonesia: What teachers learned and how. In D. Tafazoli, & M. Picard. (Eds.), *Handbook of CALL teacher education and professional development*. Springer, Singapore. https://doi.org/10.1007/978-981-99-0514-0_9

Ministry of Education of the People's Republic of China. (2020). 教育部介绍疫情期间大中小学在线教育有关情况和下一步工作考慮 [Ministry of Education briefs on online teaching during Covid-19 and plans]. Retrieved August 25, 2020, from http://www.gov.cn/xinwen/2020-05/15/content_5511824.htm

Naylor, N., & Nyanjom, J. (2021). Educators' emotions involved in the transition to online teaching in higher education. *Higher Education Research and Development, 40*(6), 1236–1250. https://doi.org/10.1080/07294360.2020.1811645

Ng, C., Yeung, A. S., & Hon, R. Y. H. (2006). Does online language learning diminish interaction between student and teacher? *Educational Media International, 43*(3), 219–232. https://doi.org/10.1080/09523980600641429

Pifarre, M. (2019). Using interactive technologies to promote dialogic space for creating collaboratively: A study in secondary education, *Thinking Skills and Creativity, 32*, 1–16. https://doi.org/10.1016/j.tsc.2019.01.004

Putri, W. (2021). E-learning pedagogical challenges of EFL teachers during COVID-19 pandemic. *EDUTECH, 20*(1), 87–97. Retrieved from https://ejournal.upi.edu/index.php/edutech/article/view/30993/pdf

Sari, D. M., Widyantoro, A., & Octavia, S. (2021). Primary school in the time of covid-19: Parents' engagement in students' online learning. *Journal Pendidikan Dan Pengajaran, 54*(2), 207–219. http://doi.org/10.23887/jpp.v54i2

Savignon, S. J. (1987). Communicative language teaching. *Theory Into Practice, 26*(4), 235–242. https://doi.org/10.1080/00405848709543281

Savignon, S. J. (1991). Communicative language teaching: State of the art. *TESOL Quarterly, 25*(2), 261–278. https://doi.org/10.2307/3587463

Spada, N., & Lightbown, P. (2009). Interaction research in second/foreign language classrooms. In A. Mackey & C. Polio (Eds.), *Multiple perspectives on interaction* (pp. 157–175). Routledge.

Swain, M. (2006). Languaging, agency and collaboration in advanced second language proficiency. In H. Byrns (Ed.), *Advanced language learning: The contribution of Halliday and Vygotsky* (pp. 95–108). Continuum.

Tare, M., Golonka, E. M., Vatz, K., Bonilla, C. L., Crooks, C., & Strong, R. (2014). Effects of interactive chat versus independent writing on L2 learning. *Language Learning & Technology, 18*(3), 208–227.

Thorne, S., Black, R., & Sykes, J. (2009). Second language use, socialization, and learning in Internet interest communities and online gaming. *The Modern Language Journal, 93*(S1), 802–821. https://doi.org/10.1111/j.1540-4781.2009.00974.x

Walker, K., & Koralesky, K. (2021). Student and instructor perceptions of engagement after the rapid online transition of teaching due to COVID-19. *Natural Sciences Education, 50*(1), 1–10. https://doi.org/10.1002/nse2.20038

Wong, R. (2020). When no one can go to school: Does online learning meet students' basic learning needs? *Interactive Learning Environments, 31*(1), 1–17. https://doi.org/10.1080/10494820.2020.1789672

Yafaei, Y., & Rais, A. (2019). Understanding teachers' integration of moodle in EFL classrooms: A case study. *English Language Teaching, 12*(4), 1–6. https://doi.org/10.5539/elt.v12n4p1

Zeng, G., & Takatsuka, S. (2009). Text-based peer–peer collaborative dialogue in a computer-mediated learning environment in the EFL context. *System, 37*(3), 434–446. https://doi.org/10.1016/j.system.2009.01.003

Zhou, Z. (2020). On the lesson design of online college English class during the COVID-19 pandemic. *Theory and Practice in Language Studies, 10*(11), 1484–1488. http://doi.org/10.17507/tpls.1011.21

Zhou, L., Wu, S., Zhou, M., & Li, F. (2020). 'School's out, but class on', the largest online education in the world today: Taking China's practical exploration during the COVID-19 epidemic prevention and control as an example. *Best Evidence of Chinese Education, 4*(2), 501–519. https://papers.ssrn.com/sol3/papers.cfm?abstract_id=3555520

Zsohar, H., & Smith, J. A. (2008). Transition from the classroom to the web: Successful strategies for teaching online. *Nursing Education Perspectives, 29*(1), 23–28.

CHAPTER 3

EXPLORING NEW ASSESSMENT SCENARIOS DURING THE PANDEMIC

The Case for Design-Based Research

Gabriel Díaz Maggioli
Universidad ORT Uruguay

ABSTRACT

Amid the COVID-19 pandemic, teachers shifted to emergency remote teaching, facing challenges in online course delivery. This chapter discusses a 2021 design based research project with student teachers in a South American national teacher education college. The project aimed to empower student teachers in assessing students' learning in the English as a Foreign Language classroom during online teaching. By addressing issues of authenticity, identity protection, and trustworthiness, the project provided a conceptual and procedural perspective on classroom research. The intervention focused on assessing communication skills, leading to a more authentic assessment of learning that considered both instructors' and students' needs.

The mandatory migration of teaching and learning to technology-mediated or technology-supported environments because of the COVID-19 pandemic has become known as emergency remote teaching (ERT). This mode of instructional delivery posed a multitude of problems to teachers, learners, and educational institutions alike. Amongst the various hurdles faced by teachers, we can also count unfamiliarity with the use of technology, inability to reach and teach all learners, lack of connectivity, lack of equipment, insufficient pedagogical preparation to migrate teaching to the online environment, and uncertainty regarding the assessment of learners' progress. As Hoadley and Campos (2022) indicate, "Online learning in the pandemic changed almost every characteristic of school as people knew it, and challenged how educators, students, and families experienced fairly established ideas such as attention, involvement, and the social connections schools typically promote" (p. 208).

The issue of assessment was particularly worrisome as it affected the actual impact of ERT on students' learning (Gamage et al., 2020; Mohd Nordin et al., 2022; Tuah & Naing, 2021). In this chapter, I see the issue of online assessment during ERT as problematic from the point of view of equitable access to quality education (Elzainy et al., 2020). In the context described in the chapter, access was not a main concern because of national connectivity policies, but access to *quality* teaching and learning was. In this sense, assessment of, for, and as learning (Díaz Maggioli, 2023b) could have been used as a learning scaffold rather than just a measuring stick. When used in this way, assessment becomes an actual tool for learning that provides relevant, live information on learning, allowing both learners and teachers to make the necessary modifications to their approaches to ascertain equal access to quality educational provisions.

In this chapter, I present a case study in Uruguay of a group of student teachers (STs) and their subject-didactics instructor (SDI) who navigated the difficult waters of assessment in English as a foreign language (EFL) classes during the COVID-19 pandemic. I start by describing the context and the participants that justify the need for this research project. Next, I explain my application of design based research as a methodology (Brown, 1992; The Design Based Research Collective, 2003) and describe how each phase of the research process was accomplished. I conclude with a discussion of results and recommendations for future research.

CONTEXT OF THE STUDY

The project was undertaken during a two-semester-long academic course at one of the campuses of the National Teacher Education Council (NTEC), the main degree-granting institution for educators in the country. In

Uruguay, teacher education is provided tuition-free in 33 campuses around the country. The initial teacher education (ITE) program lasts 4 years and includes what Cramer and Schreiber (2018) call the four essential elements of ITE "scientific disciplines (e.g., mathematics), educational sciences (e.g., educational psychology), subject didactics (e.g., subject-matter teaching and learning, such as mathematics education), and practical training (e.g., internships)" (p. 151).

In the Uruguayan system, the three first elements are organized as year-long courses on campus, while the internship (practicum) happens in schools in the catchment area of the campus. During the second and third years of study, STs undertake teaching practice under the mentorship of a cooperating teacher (CT) and the supervision of the SDI. During the fourth and final year of studies, each student teacher (ST) is assigned their own group of students in the public education system and is supported only by their SDI. In this particular year, they made the move from aspiring teachers (Díaz Maggioli, 2012) to novice teachers. This means that they are in charge of curriculum development for the first time. Some of their responsibilities are to use evidence-based tools and practices to account for their learners' learning.

During the 2021 academic year at a local branch of the NTEC, I taught and oversaw the teaching practice component of the last language pedagogy course. The group was made up of six female STs who had no previous significant teaching experience, although they had done their teaching practice under the mentorship of cooperating teachers (CTs) in a face-to-face environment one year before the pandemic, and entirely online through ERT during the first year of the pandemic.

Their level of preparation for ERT was basic in the best of cases, having received modeling from the CT and support from the CEIBAL program for only 1 year (Brovetto, 2017). CEIBAL is a national program started in 2007 in Uruguay oriented at bridging the digital divide by providing every student in the public education system with a laptop computer. Since its inception, it has also generated several digital educational resources such as the provision of an online library and a learning management system that includes regular free courses and workshops on how to use these tools. Thus, when the COVID-19 pandemic hit, Uruguay was exceptionally prepared to face it. Through cross-sectoral collaboration, free WIFI access was provided to everyone using the CEIBAL tools and equipment. Thus, there were no significant issues of access, and when issues arose, the response from local authorities was prompt. Two weeks after the lockdown was decreed, every student and teacher in the public education sector of the country had moved to ERT.

Despite this level of government support, teachers experienced a steep learning curve as they became familiar with the new technology. For example, STs in this case study suffered from a lack of both pedagogical skills for ERT and technological skills to manage and use the learning management system to its full capacity, including its videoconferencing application. To compound matters more, each school where these STs did their practicum developed its own requirements for the use of the tools available and for the organization of how classes were delivered. In some schools, STs saw their students synchronously only once a week while the rest of the time was devoted to independent student work through online forum discussions and tasks. In other schools, STs were required to teach the four weekly periods synchronously and were only allowed to use the learning management system for the submission of homework once a week.

Overall, assessment policies in the country failed to become more flexible and responsive to the needs of ERT delivery. National education authorities, for example, insisted that the assessment methods used before the pandemic (monthly written tests, project-based assessment, quizzes, oral interviews, among others) still be applied, but they did not offer teachers much support in understanding how these assessment tools could be purposefully reconfigured for the ERT context. This resulted in teachers prioritizing those assessment tools with which they felt most comfortable. It should be noted that, in this context, assessment was understood exclusively as the accreditation of students' learning and the main concern was that students did not fall behind and that syllabi were tailored to the appropriate grade level.

When working with the STs in this research project, it soon became apparent that they needed additional support from their subject didactics instructor (SDI) if they were to succeed in both teaching their students to grade expectations, and developing the necessary core practices, core skills, and core dispositions (Díaz Maggioli, 2023a) to be effective teachers. Of the six STs in the group, two voiced concerns about their inability to provide quality teaching to their learners and expressed their intention of dropping out of the college course and, consequently, their practicum group only three weeks after the ERT course had been launched. The remaining four, although not intent on dropping out, voiced their frustration at having to teach without fully understanding the potential of the tools they had at their disposal.

Because of this situation, and the fact that the pandemic presented us with an entirely new and unknown scenario, I proposed that we use our language pedagogy course to research better ways of teaching and learning. Engaging in this project would afford all STs the extra support they needed without disregarding their own needs in language teaching and learning. Concurrently, this model would allow them to develop the knowledge, skills, and dispositions they need to succeed in teaching.

Hence, the purpose of the research project was twofold. On the one hand, as an SDI, I needed to help my students fulfill their graduation requirements. On the other hand, my responsibility as a teacher educator was to facilitate their use of the necessary professional tools that would guarantee the success of the language learners in their practicum groups. Because of this context, I opted to implement a design based research (DBR) project during the 2021 course. I did this in the belief that DBR allows co-researchers to learn important situated lessons that can be applied directly to the relevant contexts to improve educational practice (Edelson, 2002). In the next section, I describe the choice of methodology, research tools, and process we undertook.

METHODOLOGY

The need to develop a targeted intervention emerged from the complexity of the pandemic situation as well as from the STs' own learning needs. However, just providing STs with the conceptual basis for effective ERT would not suffice. What was needed was an intervention that would help STs and their learners succeed. Additionally, they would be empowered by accessing professional development affordances that they would be able to use as full-fledged professionals once they graduated.

During the pandemic, we faced such intricate problems with the complexity of praxis that a straightforward problem-solving approach supported by lecturing, reading, experimentation, and reflection would not be enough to prepare student teachers for the arduous task of teaching a foreign language virtually. As Hoadley and Campos (2022) explain, problem-solving involves applying known methods to achieve a solution. However, we were faced with the dual task of identifying the most relevant problem and developing original solutions for it. Simon (1987/1995, as cited in Hoadley & Campos, 2022) distinguishes between two cognitive processes: problem-solving and design. To him, in design, "problem finding, and definition is as important as solutions, where outcomes may not be predictable, and in which a person may need to go beyond their existing repertoire of methods" (Hoadley & Campos, 2022, p. 209).

Additionally, what we were pursuing was not an academic exercise in learning to undertake research but an empirical, creative process stemming out of the need to target complex and highly situated teaching and learning problems to improve learning (Shrivastava & Shrivastava, 2021).

Given the context described above, it was decided to implement a DBR project, in the belief that "design knowledge explicitly arises from the conjunction of the general and the particular (Kali & Hoadley, 2021; Nelson & Stolterman, 2012), and can help fill the gap left by methods that depend on universality and complete generalizability" (Hoadley & Campos, 2022, p. 210).

Along the same lines, Vaezi et al. (2019) explain that DBR:

> emphasizes the link between research and practice because direct application of the theory on practice is not possible due to the existence of complex relationships between theory and practice. Therefore, researchers, educators, and practitioners must work together using DBR to identify and resolve problems and gaps and eliminate these distinctions. (p. 27)

Perhaps more importantly, DBR provided a suitable exploratory and co-constructive platform for STs to articulate their identities as both teachers and learners. Because of the nature of this research approach, they developed an awareness of the difficulties of designing and implementing effective technology-mediated educational activities and resources. In addition, they also needed to engage with axiological concerns about students' mental and physical well-being as well as the need to contextualize the aims of assessment, given pandemic-related challenges in schools (Hoadley & Campos, 2022).

To construct this research project, we followed the suggestions by Scott et al. (2020) regarding the steps of DBR. From the myriad hurdles STs were facing, we started by identifying one common problem that needed to be addressed. This was done using an online tool that allowed participants to input anonymous individual answers, thus generating a list. The original list was revised to eliminate duplicates and then we used the ranking functionality of the same online tool to agree on priorities and arrive at one problem that all STs shared as a concern (Easterday et al., 2014).

Afterward, we explored the literature (both research-based and practice-based) to identify possible "solutions." Based on this literature, we created instructional tools that would address the concern. Tools such as performance tasks were collectively created and audited against a set of criteria derived from the literature review (authenticity, constructed response, etc.).

Next, each of the participants tested the assessment artifacts co-constructed in the teacher education class in their own practicum groups and we reconvened to assess the impact of these on their learners' learning. Additionally, an electronic questionnaire (in the learners' mother tongue) was distributed to learners who responded to it right after the solution was applied. The questionnaire asked students four simple questions: how they had felt during the intervention, their opinion on the usefulness of the feedback they received after each task, what they had found easy and difficult in the tasks, and what they had learned from the process.

Following this, we revised the tools and derived situated learning from the previous phases. We looked at what worked and what did not, analyzed what did not work in detail, and tried, at all times, to see how theory supported the practices implemented and how research informed that theory. Our discussions followed a protocol created by the researcher by which each participant took turns presenting their findings, which included evidence derived from the learner questionnaires as well. Each presentation lasted for ten minutes, five of which were devoted to what worked, and the remaining five to what did not work. The rest of the group of STs then got together and generated comments and questions on the presentations. The participant whose work was on display then had five minutes to plan answers and an extra ten minutes to respond. After each presentation and question and answer session was over, one of the other participants summarized the findings and these were recorded in writing. Once all participants had presented their findings, these were systematized in a shared electronic document as lessons learned. This document was the basis for the next and final stage of the process.

Finally, we concluded and incorporated the new learning as part of the educational resources the STs would provide to learners for the rest of the semester.

The whole process took a total of 4 weeks, with our weekly online course meetings devoted to working on this project. Additionally, STs were asked to compile a portfolio of the process which included the following: a weekly reflection on the process and its implementation; draft instruments and other documents in the intervention; and an annotated bibliography of the works consulted. This portfolio was then used as an assessment tool which became part of the final assessment of the language pedagogy course.

It should be noted at this stage, that all ethical considerations associated with research with humans were taken into consideration. Informed consent was requested from co-participants and/or their parents, as well as from anyone who informed the data collection. People and institutions have been anonymized and their identities protected. Data were safeguarded electronically in external hard drives. Data were encrypted and password protected.

In the next section, I will present the results that were gathered in each of the above-mentioned phases, and discuss the findings, challenges, and potential of DBR as a tool for dialogic learning and teaching in initial teacher education programs.

DATA ANALYSIS

As it has been explained before, data emerged through the DBR cycle. Hence, it was fundamental to keep accurate records at every stage of the process. To do this, each synchronous class session was recorded. To not distract from the focus of the research, recordings were later watched again, and relevant sections of the data were transcribed to generate a database of what could be considered growth points (Johnson & Golombek, 2016). This was validated with co-participants before being coded. This same process was done with the calibration protocol and with learners' answers to the post-lesson survey.

Data were first analyzed deductively to identify instances of growth in STs' understanding of teaching and assessment. From the various categories of growth points, themes emerged. Some of the themes that emerged from the data included identifying the focus of the intervention, deciding on strategies for the intervention, monitoring the application of the intervention, and evaluating the impact of the intervention. These themes were then subject to iterative coding processes from which analytic storylines (Saldaña, 2013) helped identify results.

RESULTS

Given that DBR is a cyclical process that develops over time, both the learning derived from engaging in it and the conclusions that emerged from the whole cycle form part of the results of the investigation. I will now present the results for each of the stages in the DBR process, as well as for the final findings which constitute the evaluated and validated designed solution.

Identifying and Prioritizing the Focus Problem

As it has been explained before, an online decision-making tool was used to explore ST concerns. First, a list of all their concerns was compiled and, once that list had been cleared of duplicates and overlaps, the ranking functionality of the online tool was applied to come up with a final list of priorities. Table 3.1 shows the initial brainstorming of concerns and their final ranking.

As can be seen from the initial list of concerns, STs faced a multitude of issues related to curriculum development. Before engaging STs in a synthesis of their initial brainstorming and a ranking of their concerns to identify a single common main concern, STs were asked to explain the concerns on their list. It soon became clear that their main preoccupations were concerned mostly with effectively communicating what they were teaching well and not so much with students' learning. This is a typical concern of novice teachers (Díaz Maggioli, 2023a; Furlong & Maynard, 1995) and one that is characteristic of the problem of autonomy STs face when first having to perform in real classrooms.

On the other hand, when STs were deciding on their choice of focus for this research project, they voiced that their concern stemmed from two main sources: school authorities pressuring them to deliver results, and parents demanding changes to teaching to accommodate emotional issues their children were having because of the pandemic.

TABLE 3.1 The Initial List of Concerns Voiced by Participants and the Final Ranking

Initial Concerns Voiced by STs	Final Ranking of Concerns
Active learning.	Assessing and communicating students' learning outcomes.
Activities for online teaching.	
Combining summative and formative assessment.	Managing learners' participation and engagement.
Deciding what to test.	Enhancing active learning online.
Engaging students online.	Enhancing oral skills in online environments.
Making sure students are progressing.	
How to make grammar more interesting.	
Improving pronunciation.	
Promoting speaking.	
Providing feedback to learners.	
Increasing attendance to online classes.	
Giving students grades for participation.	
Communicating with parents and authorities.	
How to know if I am teaching well	

As one of the STs put it, "There are times when I do not know what to do, whether to concentrate on teaching or on completing the weekly plans and reports on learning results that the school Principal requires." Another ST emphasized, "I am giving grades for so many reasons that it is hard to know if I am evaluating learning, or just being a compassionate motivational caretaker."

Because of all of the above, the decision was to focus our research on creating an assessment solution that would cater to the demands for summative learning information stemming from school authorities and parents while, at the same time, allowing STs and their learners to track the progress of their actual learning. Hence, we entitled the research project: Exploring new assessment scenarios.

Designing a Prototype for the Intervention

To design a classroom-based assessment system that would yield evidence of students' actual language development in the context of ERT, the STs, guided by me, explored the available literature on authentic assessment in online environments. STs also informally interviewed colleagues in the schools where they worked and created a shortlist of "situated best practices" based on the opinions of those colleagues. Eventually, two STs also focused on the work of the American Council for the Teaching of Foreign Languages (ACTFL) on Integrated Performance Assessment (IPA; Adair-Hauck et al., 2013). While this is not strictly an online assessment system, it is a form of authentic summative assessment that could be easily adapted to an online environment, employing the tools available to STs through the online learning management system. Hence, in our research study, we decided to use an IPA approach because it presented a more authentic way of reviewing students' expression and comprehension in classroom situations. Given that it is also criterion-referenced, we were able to track the individual process of each learner and provide compensation strategies, if needed. In one of my previous research studies, I defined "integrated performance assessment (IPA) [as] a form of cluster assessment which capitalizes on the inherently intertwined nature of the three modes of communication: interpretive, interpersonal, and presentational" (Diaz Maggioli, 2020, p. 55). This form of summative assessment is organized around one or more tasks for each mode of communication, all targeting a common theme and building on one another. In this sense, it is not a formal test, in the traditional sense of a paper-and-pencil evaluation, but a series of tasks that are no different from everyday classroom tasks. The difference is that the teacher collects the tasks and grades them, providing learners with almost immediate feedback on their performance. The IPA sequence starts with a presentational task (reading or listening) on the theme selected. Learners complete these tasks as part of the lesson. The teacher collects all answers to the interpretive task and grades the work before the following lesson.

In the next lesson, the teacher returns the graded work to students and provides detailed formative feedback. Next, the teacher engages learners in an interpersonal oral interaction task which is a logical follow-up to the interpretive task performed earlier. In the context of our research project, this was done via breakout rooms with students working in pairs or trios and recording their interactions to upload their audio recordings to the learning management system. Again, STs graded the work and, in the following lesson, provided students with detailed feedback on their performance.

The final phase of IPA consists of a presentational task done individually by students after having received feedback on the interpersonal task. The presentational task may include a writing task or an oral presentation. The teacher grades this work and provides students with detailed feedback during the following lesson. These processes were undertaken by all STs in the group.

To assess the three modes of communication, the original developers of IPA designed standardized rubrics. However, in our context, the STs considered that these rubrics were far too general and did not fully represent the level of competence of their students, who were mostly at false-beginner and elementary levels of proficiency, that is, levels A1 and A2 in the Common European Framework of Reference (Council of Europe, 2020).

Hence, they decided to collaboratively design generic rubrics for each of the modes of communication with reference only to those two levels and use the descriptors found in the Common European Framework of Reference for the sake of reliability. The rubrics were shared with ELT colleagues in the STs schools who validated them and provided suggestions for improvement after piloting them with their students.

Testing of the Agreed Solution

The solution found to the problem of assessing and communicating learning was to implement an IPA sequence as part of regular instruction over a week, gather reliable data on learning through the rubrics and the documented outcomes of the tasks set, request the opinion of learners as to how this intervention had impacted them, and, finally, communicate these results to school authorities and parents.

For the implementation of this intervention, STs worked in pairs to have a critical friend throughout the process. This meant that an ST peer was present during the synchronous online classes when IPA was implemented and participated in a calibration protocol (Díaz Maggioli, 2018). This involved each participant in the online synchronous class grading the work of the learners and then coming together to share their grading and discuss similarities and differences. This was done for the sake of consistency and reliability of the grading (Yulianto & Mujtahid, 2021). This calibration protocol was undertaken during one of our synchronous online classes so that each pair would profit from the feedback of other STs and the SDI.

Revisions to the Tools

After the intervention was implemented over the same week by all STs, both the results of the calibration protocol and the answers of learners to the learner questionnaire were analyzed.

From the calibration protocol three issues surfaced:

1. Rubrics failed to account for all evidence of students' learning. In particular, an indicator of "communicative ability" was missing for the interpersonal task. While there were indicators for "accuracy" and "fluency," it was felt that learners used compensatory strategies during interactive communication (e.g., using gestures and mediating each other's expression) that could not be assessed and were integral to the success of learners in the task.
2. For the interpretive mode tasks, the rubrics were far too ambitious in relation to the learners' actual level of language development.

The way this rubric had been built was by listing microskills of listening and reading and then developing descriptors for each. Many of the microskills listed in the rubric could not be assessed or they were not readily evidenced.
3. For the presentational task, (which in our case was a writing task) questions surfaced as to the effectiveness of the instructions. While text type and purpose were clearly specified, there was no clear audience for the proposed text.

The revision of the instruments then took place, incorporating the missing elements to the rubrics and creating a checklist for the setting up of writing tasks in the future.

As far as answers to the learners' questionnaire were concerned, several interesting positive aspects were indicated:

1. Learners did not recognize the sequence of tasks as a form of assessment. STs had to explain to them, at the end of the process, that they had been evaluated. One learner pointed out "I did not know this was a test! Can we make all the tests like this?"[1]
2. Learners found the interpersonal task to be the most challenging, but they said that having the chance to record it, listen to it (an unintended consequence of the work in breakout rooms) and edit their expression was a plus. One learner explained "I don't know if it is alright, but we recorded, then listened and saw we didn't like it, so we recorded it again and uploaded it."
3. In terms of the usefulness of the feedback received after each task, there was a consensus among 78% of the learners surveyed that they profited from "the corrections and explanations that the teacher gave about what we did wrong" and that they were "able to use new words and expressions in English during the conversation that I learned in the reading we did the first day."
4. Finally, in respects to the actual learning derived from the intervention, learners mentioned mostly having learned new vocabulary, new expressions, and new information about the topic. Only three learners reported that they had learned that the way in which they said or wrote something "was wrong, but now I know how to say it and will say/write this way in the future." Another student said, "I realized how much English I know. I didn't think I knew so much English."

Findings: New Learning

Because of the dual audience and purpose in this project, it is important to say a word about the learning that STs gained from their participation in it. Evidence of their appropriation of DBR as a useful professional development tool was derived from the portfolios they presented. First and foremost, there was a requirement that all entries should have a reflective caption. Analysis showed that STs' captions became progressively more reflective as the project evolved. Their first pieces of evidence and the accompanying captions were mostly descriptive and narrative and concerned with the STs themselves as individuals. After the intervention was tested, in light of learners' answers to the questionnaires, and the collective auditing of the instruments were carried out, captions began to include elements of reflection such as: inferences from the data, critical appraisal of actions, speculations about alternative solution (with sources correctly identified), statements of commitment to implementing findings in the future, and reference to the work and reflections of their peers.

DISCUSSION

Overall, this project had two goals: to help STs assess and share their learners' learning with interested stakeholders outside the classroom, and to enable STs to appropriate a tool for their own professional development and growth. The means to attain these goals was to implement a DBR project that would allow STs to identify a particular concern relevant to both their teaching and their learners' learning, and to design an innovative solution to that concern.

Analysis of the data indicated that the project attained both goals. From the point of view of STs, they became aware of an innovative approach to summative assessment, and they appropriated it by contextualizing and adapting it to their current situational context. In the process, they developed core concepts about assessment, learning and teaching in ERT situations. Simultaneously, they were able to gather evidence of learners' learning of English through written texts, audio recordings, written feedback comments and learners' written expressions. They were also able to develop collaborative skills in terms of supporting one another throughout the research process, critically appraising their own work and that of their peers and learners, and, more importantly, gaining confidence and control of their teaching.

The learning outcomes of the project for STs indicate that they have been able to decenter from the egocentric positioning of the novice (Furlong & Maynard, 1995) on teaching alone, and focus on learners and their learning. Additionally, they became more keenly aware of the communicative ability of learners at the A1 and A2 levels and managed to design, edit, and improve educational artifacts that focused primarily on evidence of learning.

They also were able to appropriate core practices that teaching professionals exhibit such as collaborative work and developing an inquiring approach to the conundrums of teaching and learning. These conundrums constitute the daily fare of teaching as we are presented with multiple decision-making processes during any regular teaching day. These decisions sometimes come from our prior experience as teachers and learners, thus not necessarily suitable for our current group of students. However, being able to pose questions, explore possibilities, and collaboratively generate solutions with the opportunity to reflect on their outcomes, allowed STs to become more sensitive to the context and the context-appropriate pedagogy that was needed.

Learners also learned from their participation in this research process. They developed new understandings about language learning, the teacher's actions, the power of assessment, and their own language learning. They also acted as co-participants by providing useful insights into how the intervention affected them and their learning. One of the ethical mandates of this research project was that its implementation should result in a benefit to learners and their learning, not just a benefit to STs. In this sense, every learner's individual situation was taken into consideration. At the same time, the project yielded relevant authentic data regarding learning which allowed STs to make the necessary adjustments to their instruction to ascertain everyone's success.

This process of adaptation is a key characteristic of knowledge generation at this early stage in the career development of novice instructors. The many layers and types of design implemented in light of the situational characteristics of the context allowed for a more in-depth understanding, both of core professional concepts and their related core professional attributes. The implementation of the intervention gave rise to different modes of doing assessment and allowed STs to develop a deeper sensitivity towards their learners and their own concerns. Moreover, learners were able to reflect on their own learning of the language while also developing new learning strategies.

Finally, as a teacher educator and researcher, I was also afforded the chance to learn and develop. Firstly, I learned that identifying a problem is not a straightforward decision, but a process which requires dialogue, negotiation, and reflection. Secondly, I learned that DBR can act as a powerful awareness-raising and pedagogical development tool for novice teachers when undertaken in the context of a community of practice like this project. Lastly, I learned that mediated learning activity does not only require expert mediation, but also peer-mediation, learner-mediation, and self-mediation. Each of these dimensions of mediation enriches the research process and the learning that stems from it.

Having clarified the advantages of this DBR project, I now address its limitations. Both DBR as a research methodology and this particular DBR project can be identified as possessing limitations. One key limitation considers the fact that this project focused on the design of one intervention and that, given the low number of participants, only one iteration of the DBR cycle was needed. In addition, the results presented here cannot be generalized because of how contextually bound they are. Finally, a limitation worth highlighting is that there was no methodological certainty that the time and approach to the redesign of the intervention was sufficient. Vaezi et al. (2019) specify that

> DBR does not specify the number of steps needed to improve design and subsequent evaluations and it is difficult to determine whether the design cycle is already completed or will be completed later. For this reason, confidence in the capability of extending the results to other research will not be certain. (p. 32)

Nevertheless, in the context of this particular project, DBR became a useful tool for the SDI, six STs, and their learners to design a solution to a complex situation that needed an answer. Additionally, DBR acted as a conceptual tool for STs to understand their learners and their own learning better and provided them with affordances (evidence) to make claims about that learning.

CONCLUSIONS

The COVID-19 pandemic affected all realms of life and education was not an exception. Teachers were overexerted and had to reinvent the way they taught overnight, without much support in many cases. However, even in cases where that support was available, the complexity of the situation demanded that teachers seek answers to problems they had never faced before. Hence, DBR, with its emphasis on understanding the audience and gearing the design to their specific needs, became a principled intervention that allowed co-participants to give a response to the problem which was satisfactory for all stakeholders involved.

In future research, it would be interesting to track the participants in this iteration of this research project and find out whether DBR promoted a true change in their knowledge, skills, and disposition, or simply remained limited to something accomplished in the context of ERT. Additionally, it would be interesting to find out whether these STs are using DBR as tool for ongoing professional development, now that they are full-fledged teaching professionals.

NOTE

1. Translation from Spanish into English by the author.

REFERENCES

Adair-Hauck, B., Glisan, E. W., & Trojan, F. J. (2013). *Implementing integrated performance assessment*. American Council for the Teaching of Foreign Languages.

Brovetto, C. (2017). Language policy and language practice in Uruguay: A case of innovation in English language teaching in primary schools. In L. Khami-Stein, G. Díaz Maggioli., & L. de Oliveira (Eds.), *English language teaching in South America: Policy, preparation and practice* (pp. 75–91). Multilingual Matters.

Brown, A. L. (1992). Design experiments: Theoretical and methodological challenges in creating complex interventions in classroom settings. *Journal of the Learning Sciences, 2*(2), 141–178. https://doi.org/10.1207/s15327809jls0202_2

Council of Europe. (2020). *Common European framework for languages: Learning, teaching, assessment*. Companion Volume. https://rm.coe.int/common-european-framework-of-reference-for-languages-learning-teaching/16809ea0d4

Cramer, C., & Schreiber, F. (2018). Subject didactics and educational sciences: Relationships and their implications for teacher education from the viewpoint of educational sciences. *Research In Subject-matter Teaching and Learning, 1*(1), 150–164. https://doi.org/10.23770/rt1818

Díaz Maggioli, G. (2012). *Teaching language teachers: Scaffolding professional learning*. Rowman & Littlefield Education.

Díaz Maggioli, G. (2018). Writing calibration. In J. I. Liontas (Ed.), *The TESOL encyclopedia of English language teaching* (pp. 5329–5333). John Wiley & Sons.

Díaz Maggioli, G. (2020). Integrated performance assessment as an interface between learning and assessment. In S. Hibri (Ed.), *Changing language assessment: New dimensions, new challenges* (pp. 53–73). Springer.

Díaz Maggioli, G. (2023a). *Initial language teacher education*. Routledge.

Díaz Maggioli, G. (2023b). Authentic assessment of, for, and as learning. In S. Spezzini & V. Canese (Eds.), *Teaching English in global contexts: Language, learners, and learning*. Editorial Facultad de Filosofía, Universidad Nacional de Asunción.

Easterday, M. W., Rees Lewis, D., & Gerber, E. M. (2014). Design-based research process: Problems, phases and applications. In J. Polman, E. A. Kyza, D. K. O'Neill, I. Tabak, W. R. Penuel, A. S. Jurow, K. O'Connor, T. Lee, & L. D'Amico (Eds.), *Learning and becoming in practice: The international conference of the learning sciences* (pp. 317–324). International Society of the Learning Sciences.

Edelson, D. E. (2002) Design research: What we learn, when we engage in design. *Journal of the Learning Sciences, 11*(1), 105–121. https://doi.org/10.1207/S15327809JLS1101_4

Elzainy, A., El Sadik, A., & Al Abdulmonem, W. (2020). Experience of e-learning and online assessment during the COVID-19 pandemic at the College of Medicine, Qassim University. *Journal of Taibah University Medical Sciences 15*(6), 256–462. https://doi.org/10.1016/j.jtumed.2020.09.005

Furlong, J., & Maynard, T. (1995). *Mentoring student teachers. The growth of professional knowledge*. Routledge.

Gamage, K. A. A., de Silva, E. K., & Gunawardhana, N. (2020). Online delivery and assessment during COVID-19: Safeguarding academic integrity. *Education Sciences, 10*(11) 1–24. https://doi.org/10.3390/educsci10110301

Hoadley, C., & Campos, F. C. (2022). Design-based research: What it is and why it matters to studying online learning. *Educational Psychologist, 57*(3), 207–220. https://doi.org/10.1080/00461520.2022.2079128

Johnson, K. E., & Golombek, P. (2016). *Mindful L2 teacher education: A sociocultural perspective on cultivating teachers' professional development*. Routledge.

Kali, Y. & Hoadley, C. (2021). Design-based research methods in CSCL: Calibrating our epistemologies and ontologies. In U. Cress, C. Rosé, A. Wise, & J. Oshima (Eds.), *International handbook of computer-supported collaborative learning*. Springer.

Mohd Nordin, N. R., Omar, W., & Mohd Ridzuan, N. I. (2022). Challenges and solutions on online teaching and assessment during COVID-19. *World Journal of English Language, 12*(8), 410–419. https://doi.org/10.5430/wjel.v12n8p410

Saldaña, J. (2013). *The coding manual for qualitative researchers* (2nd ed.). SAGE.

Scott, E. E., Wenderoth, M. P., & Doherty, J. (2020). Design-based research: A methodology to extend and enrich biology education research. *CBE Life Sciences in Education, 19*(3), *19*(11), 1–12. https://doi.org/10.1187/cbe.19-11-0245

Shrivastava, S., & Shrivastava P. (2021). Adoption of a design-based research approach to improve understanding about complex educational problems. *Ibnosina Journal of Medical and Biomedical Science, 13*(2), 51–53.

The Design Based Research Collective. (2003). Design-based research: An emerging paradigm for educational inquiry. *Educational Researcher, 32*(1), 5–8. https://doi.org/10.3102/0013189X032001005

Tuah, N. A. A., & Naing, L. (2021). Is online assessment in higher education institutions during COVID-19 pandemic reliable? *Siriraj Medical Journal, 73*(1), 61–68. https://doi.org/10.33192/Smj.2021.09

Vaezi, H., Moonaghi, H. K., & Golbaf, R. (2019). Design-based research: Definition, characteristics, application and challenges. *Journal of Education in Black Sea Region, 5*(1), 26–35. https://doi.org/10.31578/jebs.v5i1.185

Yulianto, D., & Mujtahid, N. M. (2021). Online assessment during COVID-19 pandemic: EFL teachers' perspectives and their practices. *Journal of English Teaching 7*(2), 229–242. https://doi.org/10.33451/jet.v7i2.2770

CHAPTER 4

FLEXIBILITY IN TEACHING DURING THE PANDEMIC

An Action-Research Study of a University Foreign Language Classroom

María Eugenia Lozano
Barnard College

ABSTRACT

Before the COVID-19 pandemic, the Spanish Department utilized midterm and final exams, comprising multiple-choice questions, closed reading exercises, and writing or listening tasks. The department was in the process of adopting a new textbook when the pandemic necessitated a redesign of course evaluations. A committee, including the author, was already exploring new assessment ideas as the shift to online teaching was announced. The chapter delves into the flexibility introduced by incorporating unit wrap-up activities, such as quizzes in the Canvas course management system, tailored for the online environment. It highlights the formative assessment derived from class projects, prioritizing students' understanding of grammar, vocabulary, and cultural content over specific details. The outcomes were positive for both students and faculty. The chapter includes critical reflections from students and faculty on this new, flexible teaching format, the evaluation process, and its impact on language learning during uncertain times.

Teaching and learning during the pandemic have expanded our understanding of what counts as knowledge, who gets to learn, who gets to teach, and the best learning and teaching practices and processes. The new online environments (e.g., Zoom, Google Meet, etc.) made us question the traditional ways of behaving both as an instructor and a student. From Zoom class etiquette, and turns at talk in an online environment, to questioning how to teach, what to do in the online class, and how to evaluate, we were questioning ourselves constantly as we were deciphering how to teach online during a pandemic. Some instructors even started questioning their choice of profession due to the countless systemic challenges in our field. Indeed, once educational institutions decided that face-to-face instruction was no longer possible, the idea of teaching in a new and imposed remote fashion had to be different from regular face-to-face teaching, and we only had a few days to figure it all out.

This chapter aims to discuss some of the limitations and the affordances the new online environment brought to the classroom dynamics, but more importantly, to describe the changes a Spanish department in a private Ivy League institution made to meet the challenges of this online environment due to the pandemic, specifically those related to formative assessment. By analyzing students' and faculty's critical reflections on such a new and flexible evaluation format, this chapter provides evidence revealing the positive impact of collaborative work to improve the assessment in a language program.

This action research study is defined by Gilmore et al. (1986) as "learning by doing" (p. 162) and entails: being able to identify a problem and do something to resolve it. It aims to contribute both to the practical concerns of people in an immediate problematic situation and to further the goals of social science simultaneously. Under this methodology, there is a strong element of collaboration among members of the community in identifying the problem and seeking possible solutions.

The following section will focus on the recent studies that have documented the state of education during and after the pandemic.

LITERATURE REVIEW: AN OVERVIEW OF KEY RESEARCH STUDIES

Some researchers have recently started to study the impact of the pandemic on pre-K to 12th-grade teacher burnout and its effects on teaching efficacy in an online environment (Pressley & Ha, 2021), Internet accessibility and (in)proper technology access for students (Simmons, 2020), and on the inflexibility of school, institutions to embrace rapid organizational change (Kraft et al., 2021). Among the results presented in these studies, the researchers found that teachers who were providing all virtual instruction had the lowest instruction and engagement efficacies. A study by Pressley (2021) concluded that there were no significant differences in teaching efficacy based on teacher location, technology familiarity, previous accolades, or teaching level, suggesting it was not a matter of the teacher's training or abilities, but rather the online environment itself and/or the student's disposition for learning that got in the way. This study concluded that anxieties related to COVID-19-related and teaching demands, issues with parent communication, and proper administrative support were key factors in determining teachers' burnout. The burnout resulted in a teaching exodus between 18% and 30% for new teachers with less than 5 years of experience, and 8% for more experienced teachers. The study also mentioned that the teaching environment played a critical role in maintaining teachers' sense of success. Teachers who received professional development that supported virtual instruction and had opportunities to collaborate with other teachers had a stronger sense of success.

Within a similar line of inquiry, Simmons (2020) reflected on how the pandemic magnified the inequities in our school systems—and in our society—that were invisible or silenced for most of us. Many students did not have the necessary tools for distance learning, including reliable internet service. Educators for Excellence (2020) found that just 51% of teachers in high-poverty schools reported that most of their students were able to participate daily in distance learning, in comparison with 84% of teachers in affluent schools. Also, many of the online learning options did not consider children who were hard of hearing, visually impaired, physically challenged, or had developmental needs. Another aspect of disparity emerged from the fact that many students did not have the support of their caregivers as they had to go out and work, leaving children by themselves, or not having the necessary skills to be able to help kids with school assignments. Simmons also presented the reality of many students who rely on schools for the most essential need: to access the food and basic daily support that was limited during the pandemic.

In a report of a survey of 600 pre-K to 12th-grade teachers across the United States presented by the organization Educators for Excellence (2020), they found out that teachers whose schools struggled to provide strong remote working conditions reported lower levels of success before the pandemic, they also experienced meaningfully larger declines in their sense of success on average. One major concern among teachers was the way the decisions were taken when making changes in the schools. Based on this survey results, a strong majority of teachers believe layoff decisions should be based on multiple factors, including both performance and seniority and prioritize cuts that do the least harm to students. In general, the report concluded that teachers' main objective was to help students cope and move forward academically, support those with special needs at home, and plan for future school closures.

Even though the circumstances can be very similar among pre-K to 12th-grade teachers and university-level instructors, they can also differ in many ways. However, there are few studies conducted focusing on the university student's point of view regarding the online environment. A study published by Turan and colleagues in 2022, conducted on 1,760 university students from 28 different universities to investigate students' perceptions of flexibility, self-regulated effort, and satisfaction with the distance education process, and their views on distance education found that the students' flexibility of time management and flexibility of content levels were quite high. The online environment allowed the students to structure their learning processes whenever, wherever, and for as long as they wanted in the online learning process. The students also mentioned the advantages of online education, such as flexibility, material richness, reduced costs, and recording of online courses. These results can be interpreted as the fact that the students adopted and applied the advantages of online learning, such as flexibility, time and place independence, and repeatability of lessons and resources.

There were a couple of studies that presented the students' difficulties during the online learning environment. Difficulties such as independent learning, time management, and maintaining motivation in the online learning process and problems such as accessibility, digital division, and inequality (Lee et al., 2021; Shin & Hickey, 2020) were common among university students. The findings of these studies indicated limitations such as the problem of accessing the courses due to the technical infrastructure, the increased workload, the lack of communication with the instructor and peers, and insufficient instructional materials.

Among the very few studies focusing on perceptions of the impact of COVID-19 on education at the college level, none of them focuses on students' and faculty's critical perceptions of the changes made to assess students in an online environment. Specifically, on how the new and multimodal forms of evaluating validate (or not) students' and faculty's learning experience, which is what the present study aims to contribute.

THE ZOOM CLASSES

In March 2020, the administration at my university sent us off to our 1-week spring break with the idea that students were not coming back to campus. They canceled the study abroad spring courses and told us we were moving to remote teaching, all of this during that same week, due to the outbreak of the COVID-19 pandemic. They also told the students they could not come back to campus and told us—the faculty—that we were going to have an extra week to prepare for online learning. It was a very stressful time, to say the least. Like most of my colleagues, I have never taught an online class, much less taken one.

When the university announced its "plan" (more like a rough idea) for teaching during the pandemic, they informed us that it was until the end of the semester and that we would come back for the fall session in person again. As my way of approaching this uncertainty, during the following 2 weeks, I attended every single workshop offered on campus in preparation for what was coming. This included creating an account on Zoom, learning how to use it, and getting familiar with different applications to be able to replicate some of the classroom dynamics in the virtual world. As I was getting ready for the unknown, fearing what the future would hold for us, I was hearing my colleagues saying on these Zoom preparation meetings that they were planning to continue using the same teaching material (i.e., PowerPoint presentations, exams, readings, etc.) as usual and that they did not think they needed to drastically change their teaching style in the new online environment, especially since it was going to be temporary. This led me to reflect deeply on my positionality and prompted a strong sense of urgency to reshape my teaching paradigm.

As soon as we were able to set up Zoom sessions on our Canvas platform, our learning management system, and we had concluded the basic training, we started having online classes, seeing our students on our computer screens represented in little squares. It was obvious from the first week of Zoom classes how inequitable the new system was. On one hand, students differed in connectivity issues so, for some, the class would go smoothly, for others, their call would get disconnected, and they would have to connect several times during a class period. Also, while some students were trying to find a background that would not reveal their living situation, others were showing off their homes, bedrooms, and outdoor landscapes. These situations made it hard to start our course content right away. It seemed impossible to have "normal classes" when the whole world was starting to face a terrifying pandemic, and everyone began their Zoom journey at a different starting point. Fortunately (one positive aspect before moving to online classes in March), we have had a couple of months to get to know each other in person, to build a group connection and class community that helped ease the transition. I came to value this in the following semesters when we started teaching fully online without having this initial first face-to-face contact, which made it very difficult to create a sense of a class community.

Affordances and Limitations of the Zoom Environment

After dealing with the initial shock of the Zoom classes for the first few days, I started to see some of the positive aspects of it. The online environment seemed to bring tools that would help accommodate students with diverse needs. At the beginning of the Zoom experience, I started noticing the quiet students in the face-to-face class were actively participating by using the online chat feature. They always had comments that were relevant to the class and seemed to be more engaged in a different way than in our previous in-person class. It took me a while to be able to manage the chat and deliver my lesson at the same time, but once I was doing it, the class started to feel more interactive than ever. Another feature that had a positive impact on my class right away was the breakout rooms. I set up the Zoom application to group students randomly and as such, students were interacting with every other student in the class in a given week. This helped maintain the community we started having before going virtual and students began to feel more comfortable with each other by the end of the semester. Another aspect that made a positive impact on the students was the recording of all of our classes. The university set up the Zoom sessions in Canvas for all the faculty so the classes were recorded and put in a class folder. Faculty who did not want their classes recorded could turn this option off. Students in my classes had access to these recordings at any time and they were able to reference them if they had questions. Additionally, when students were absent, they could watch the class on their own time. Contrary to some of the fears some faculty members had, students were still regularly attending their classes, and having the class recordings available was taken as an additional opportunity to review the material if students chose to do so.

Once we settled in with the technology, we started to move on with the material that needed to be covered during the rest of the semester. I started using the plethora of online tools I have learned about in the workshops given by the university, including Padlet, Jamboard, and Hypothes.is, StoryBoard, StoryMaps, among others. Students also began to use the tools, some of them successfully, but others could not use them due to technical limitations to their computers (e.g., lack of microphones) or their weak Internet connection. To make matters worse, the university adopted a policy where students were asked to turn their cameras on while in class. This meant students whose Internet connection was weak, could be disconnected from the class at any minute and they would have to connect again, making them miss class several times during a certain period. Some students did not have any technical disadvantages and were not using their cameras for personal reasons. Even though our university created a document called "Expectations in Our Online Classroom Community" where students were given 11 principles to follow while on Zoom, such as turning on their camera, being dressed as if going to class in person, being mindful of their surroundings, being aware of their microphone, raising their virtual hand to participate in class, not eating, and being patient with connectivity issues, among others; some students would ignore these principles and would keep their cameras off or "attend class" while going on the subway, or be laying down in their bed. At the beginning I felt like I needed to be the Zoom police, reminding students of the university expectations, making sure they were being respectful of their classmates and mindful of the online environment. It took me a few weeks to realize my students, the same as me, were struggling with this new reality and needed time to process it all. This meant that sometimes they needed to avoid certain rules and take their time to process the information or play with the technology (e.g., virtual backgrounds in Zoom) to feel comfortable in the online setting. I took the position that as long as they were coming to class and participating actively and trying to learn, they would not get penalized for not turning their cameras on. While still requiring timely submission of all class assignments, expressing my understanding and empathy towards their challenges allowed me to foster an environment of flexibility. This approach empowered students to engage in the course and contribute according to their capacities and challenges.

Changes on Assessment

Midterm and final exams were the norm in our pre-COVID-19 pandemic language courses in our Spanish Department. The two cumulative exams consisted of multiple-choice questions on the vocabulary and grammar studied throughout the semester, close reading exercises, and a writing task or listening comprehension as a way to showcase the student's abilities. When the pandemic hit us, our department was adopting a new textbook and there was a need to re-design the course assessments as well. By the time we went online, I was part of a committee along with several other colleagues[1] that oversaw redesigning the assessment component of our language program. This came at a critical moment because most of our faculty was already questioning what they were doing and trying to come up with new ideas on how to assess students' performance.

Before moving into online teaching, we had already created an assessment for a regular semester that consisted of a midterm and a final exam based on the newly adopted textbook. The format was similar to the previous ones we had had for years, and most people felt comfortable keeping things the way they were. However, when we went online, considering this new environment we were going to be in, we did not see a purpose of having closed-answer types of questions, either multiple choice or fill-in-the-blank assessments, not even written compositions. Since students were going to have all the digital materials and online tools at their disposal, we needed to create a different type of assessment that did not rely on one single correct answer. What we decided to do instead was to take into account all the new tools that were available to us, such as Panopto (a tool that allows students to create video recordings directly on Canvas), and the breakout rooms feature in Zoom, and decided to create a more comprehensive and formative assessment in the form of projects, where students could display their knowledge of a particular topic and grammatical concepts putting into practice what they have learned during each chapter, rather than focus on a single correct answer. The assessment per chapter would take the form of class projects, in which the process and students' understanding of the grammar, vocabulary, and cultural content were more important than the accuracy of a particular verb conjugation or word spelling.

We established as a committee that we needed to create reading, writing, listening, and speaking activities that involved collaborative work and with topics strictly related to the class, and to the students' personal lives, to keep the content as specific as possible to the class culture and in this way eliminate the need to bring materials or copy an assignment from outside sources. For example, students in the Spanish Elementary I class needed to interview each other about their personal information and write a dialogue to share with the whole class by the end of the activity.

As a committee, we also proposed (and received the support of the other faculty members) that instead of having a mid-term and a final exam, equivalent to 40% of the final grade, we would have a unit wrap-up after every chapter. In every semester from elementary to intermediate levels, we teach five chapters a semester, so we designed 5-unit wrap-ups for each level that were now equivalent to 50% of the final grade, with no midterm or final exams. Each chapter lasts approximately two weeks, and each wrap-up was to be taken during the last day of the chapter. During these wrap-ups students needed to produce videos, audio, and scripts, to practice the vocabulary and grammar structures learned during the particular chapter.

The Spanish Elementary Class Wrap-Up Activities

For the Elementary Spanish classes, we designed materials that were specific to the content of the new textbook we were using. For example, for the first chapter wrap-up which included personal information (name, age, personality traits) students were asked to watch an authentic video of a person auditioning for an acting role in which the person gave their name, age, personality description, and acting experience. Students needed to answer basic questions about what they heard and saw. For their writing portion of the wrap-up, students were asked to work in pairs and write a letter introducing themselves to a study abroad program and requesting information. The specific prompt was:

> Imagine you are applying to a study abroad program and you would like to introduce yourself to someone from the host university. Write a dialogue with a partner in which you ask questions that include the following information. (120–150 words)
> - First and last name
> - Age and city of origin, place of residence
> - Studies, areas of Interest
> - Email and phone number
> - Reasons for waiting *to go on an exchange*

They also had the option of recreating a video (similar to the one they had watched already) in which the students needed to introduce themselves for an acting audition. In another chapter in which they were learning about the university campus spaces, in the wrap-up activity students needed to talk about their favorite place in the university. They needed to submit a three-minute video or audio file to Canvas describing the place they chose, talking about its location, its function, activities that can be done there, describing the furniture available in the space, colors, etc. Students were given the option of working individually or in pairs for this activity that would take place outside of the classroom. Asking students to rely on their local environment and create material using the immediate resources, in this case, their university campus, demands the students to create original material that features them and their skills, and to communicate in Spanish for a real-life purpose.

Final Course Project for Elementary Spanish

In the first semester of the Elementary Spanish final course project, students are asked to work on a linguistic landscapes (LL) photo essay. The main objective of the project is for students to become aware of their surroundings by capturing signs in Spanish around their neighborhood (i.e., bus stop advertisements, publicity of any kind, store names, etc.) to ground their interpretations of the social, cultural, and political situation of immigrant communities in New York City as "situated signs-in-space" (Blommaert, 2013). At the beginning of the semester, students are given the task of collecting a series of 10 pictures of signs in Spanish around their neighborhoods (see Lozano et al., 2020 for a detailed focus of the project). This linguistic landscape project has the objective of creating awareness of the presence of the Spanish language around their city and at the same time train students to read texts critically. Once students have the 10 pictures, they need to upload them in a class Padlet (see Figure 4.1), so they end up with a pool of around 150 pictures total (15 students in a class) that shows the Hispanic culture in some way in

Figure 4.1 Padlet for Spanish 1101—Elementary Spanish I, Fall 2022.

their local and immediate community. With all the pictures available in the class Padlet, students take time during class to examine all of them and select possible topics for their essays based on those images. Their topics needed to emerge strictly from the photographs posted by the students in the class Padlet. By making this a requirement, students need to use the class material as their main source for their photo essays, instead of searching online or elsewhere for material for their final project. They need to select 5 to 6 pictures to use in their photo essay. Finally, in addition to including the pictures with a photo caption, they also need to write an introduction, a paragraph for each picture selected, and a conclusion. Among the linguistic demands of this project, since this is the first semester of Spanish, students are asked to make use of the present tense to write their essays and to use verbs to talk about location, state, and descriptions.

During their final presentation, students provided examples of the ethnographic work of their linguistic landscape projects, where they reflected on the complexity of the connections between language and culture, as well as the way they interpreted the visual and verbal codes found in an advertisement; and they problematized the messages found in these signs where cultural and social identities come in contact. For example, during the Fall 2022 semester, one student picked the topic of Hispanic food trucks in New York (Figure 4.2). Since several students had uploaded pictures of food trucks, this student decided to focus on them and research this topic, after mentioning the boom of food trucks in our neighborhood, she mentioned the problem that exists among the food vendors:

Imagen 2: Un camión de comida mexicana. Dirección: Ciento quince y Broadway

Figure 4.2   Student photo of food truck on 115th Street and Broadway, New York City.

"Para muchos inmigrantes, la venta ambulante es una de las únicas opciones para empleo. En lugar de apoyar a estas personas, NY los criminaliza. Hoy organizaciones como "The Street Vendor Project" luchan contra este problema, uniendo más que dos mil vendedores para impulsar un cambio permanente."

[For many immigrants, selling on the streets is one of the only options for employment. Instead of helping these people, NY criminalizes them. Today, organizations like "The Street Vendor Project" fight against this problem, unionizing more than two thousand workers to create a permanent change].

As a conclusion the student mentioned a similar situation of the food trucks in LA, describing a new law that came into effect this past September 30th that made it easier to obtain a selling permit. She ends her essay by saying: *"Si California puede hacerlo, nosotros también!"* [If California can do it, we can too!].

Students' Perceptions of the Wrap-Ups

Changing the evaluation from 40% pre-pandemic to 50% during the pandemic brought a lot of questions to our faculty committee. We were not sure if going from two exams to five formative assessments throughout the semester would be overwhelming for the students and the faculty. What we did not expect was that implementing the five wrap-ups would result in other changes in the curriculum as well. By doing ongoing non-cumulative assessments, we were eliminating the written compositions we had during previous pre-pandemic semesters. These compositions were now embedded in the wrap-ups and students were doing almost the same amount of writing as in a regular semester. So, from the instructor's perspective, the amount of work spent correcting exams vs. wrap-ups was going to be very similar. It also meant that instead of having a midterm during the semester (usually one class day at the mid-semester mark), now we needed to arrange 5 days for a wrap-up during the semester, which ended up meaning we spent one fewer day on each chapter.

In an anonymous survey conducted with students in the fall of 2021 where some students had gone to at least one semester pre-pandemic and had had the experience of midterms and finals, and a similar one during the Fall of 2022 where the student had only experienced the wrap-ups, 100% of students expressed they liked the wrap-ups better than the midterm and final exams. Students mentioned the new assessment incentivizes learning throughout the semester, rather than cramming all the studying the night before the exams. They expressed that they were studying more often and more consistently and that they did not feel they were falling behind on vocabulary and grammar concepts because they were being tested on what they just finished reviewing and the content had a logical progression. Moreover, several students mentioned that the midterms and finals felt very overwhelming compared to the wrap-ups which were less stress-inducing, and that they had fun completing the projects. The collaborative aspect of the wrap-ups also made the task more manageable. Having the option to work in groups makes the wrap-up more of a collaborative effort where students negotiate among themselves, trying to come up with the best way to express themselves focusing on the end product and for a real-life purpose.

In general, students mentioned the wrap-ups kept them engaged throughout the semester breaking the new content into smaller manageable pieces. These unit wrap-ups serve as checkpoints throughout the semester, so they know how they are doing on a particular chapter and what needs to be reviewed before moving to the next one.

When asked about the negative aspects of the wrap-ups, students mentioned they felt that sometimes they were being evaluated on grammatical aspects they just had learned and that they did not have the time to practice them for them to fully grasp the new concepts. They also mentioned that it could be stressful to have an exam every two or three weeks, but that since they had the same structure, the predictability made them more manageable.

Faculty Perceptions of the Wrap-Ups

For the most part, faculty have been supportive of the changes in assessment developed by the assessment committee. Most instructors welcomed the idea of having smaller non-cumulative tests during the semester rather than the two cumulative and high-stakes assessments consisting of a midterm and final. We, on the committee, presented the wrap-ups as proposals that can be modified when needed. We agreed that, as long as we all keep the same structure and duration, types of questions, and similar topics, we can swap one reading for another, one video for another, one writing task for another, and so on. So, one faculty member can decide that after watching a video of a student giving a tour of their dorm as part of the audiovisual comprehension session, for example, their students could create a similar video as part of the oral production section, instead of submitting an audio recording of a dialogue in pairs about their favorite part of the university.

When discussing the wrap-ups during faculty meetings, they mentioned that they liked the flexibility we have to be able to modify the wrap-ups according to their class needs. Others mentioned that it is important for all sessions of Spanish classes (around 62 sessions of 15 students each) to keep the same structure and consistency and that the wrap-ups provide that structure. This consistency from one level to the next level (e.g., from Elementary Spanish I to Elementary Spanish II) with different instructors, will make the transition easier for students since they will have the same course components, exam structure, and similar wrap-up content structures.

One major difference some faculty noted about the wrap-ups of the midterm and final was that there was no pressure for "covering" the material before the exams as we had before. Students know what they are going to be assessed on. The anxiety that builds up for having the exams is almost eliminated with the implementation of the wrap-ups (see Salehi & Marefat, 2014 for a study on Foreign Language Anxiety). Students during the wrap-ups do not ask the question "What is going to be in the exam?" because they know exactly that it is about the material from the chapter we just finished. Some instructors also believe that having 5 exams (wrap-ups) instead of 2 creates a lower-stakes environment that helps students bring down the exam anxiety. Students know that they will have more opportunities to improve their performance if the first wrap-up does not go as well as they expected. Another reason why faculty like using the wrap-ups is because they believe that by giving them during class time, students are less likely to use outside Internet resources (i.e., online translators) and that they will spend more time trying to work collaboratively with a partner and produce their material. However, just a couple of our senior instructors in our program were reluctant to use the wrap-ups. They expressed they did not like the formatting of the questions in some of them, or they believed that they were too difficult or too easy depending on the wrap-up the instructor selected, so they preferred to create their assessments that consisted of interactive content based on other platforms like Genial.ly (https://genial.ly/) or create modules in Canvas where students have to complete several tasks before they move to the next assignment.

A disadvantage of the wrap-ups is the need to update them constantly. We have an expanding bank of questions that rotate every semester, although fortunately, we are getting suggestions for new questions for the items banks from our faculty that have adopted new material that will be shared with the whole faculty. This means that the committee needs to work constantly to get the materials, organize them in the style of similar questions, evaluate the level of difficulty for the questions, and make sure the questions and answers are strictly related to the content of each chapter. At the same time, the continuous updating of our assessments allows our committee and our colleagues to collaborate to include new content for some of the chapter themes such as environmental issues and climate change, immigration, emerging technologies, education and careers, visual and performing arts, health care and medicine, which do change regularly.

Embracing Flexibility: Resources to Move Our Work Forward

While we were teaching during the first part of the pandemic, our university sent several emails asking instructors to be lenient and practice flexibility in our teaching. Since flexibility could take different forms depending on the class we were teaching, the Center for Engaged Pedagogy (CEP) at Barnard College under the direction of Dr. Jennifer Rosales (https://cep.barnard.edu/) organized a conference where Alex Pitman, the senior associate director of the CEP invited Barnard College faculty, Virinda Condillac from the English department, Jessica Goldstein from biology, Alice Reagan from theater and myself, all Barnard college faculty, to talk about what flexibility looks like in our classrooms for which my conference talk is the basis for this article. The name of the event was "Flexibility, Accessibility, and Equity in Course and Syllabus Design" for which they invited faculty to reflect on how one or all of the principles of flexibility, accessibility, and equity inform their approaches to designing various aspects of their courses, from specific sections of the syllabus to lesson plans, rubrics, and more. Several instructors talked about the balance between being lenient with students' needs without compromising their own educational standards or those of the university. They gave examples of modifications they made starting with the course syllabus and taking away the weight that class discussions had as the primary teaching tool in an English class for example, due to the inconsistent engagement of the students in a day-to-day and switching it to a more hands-on work during class to try to keep students engaged. They also talk about planning several shorter activities during a particular class period and keeping the activities consistent to create a familiarity and routine that can help ease students' anxiety. Additionally, they mentioned that it was important to talk about the class's objectives very clearly at the beginning of the lesson to give a sense of direction for the class and, at the same time, to give students a sense of completion at the end of it. One of the ideas about modifying the assignments was to give students several assignments to choose from or to allow them to propose their own assignments that will fulfill the course objectives and or requirements. It also became obvious that students needed scaffolding to finish their assignments, so some instructors created process-based rubrics rather than product-based ones as a way to incentivize the steps taken to get toward the final class project. This creation on process-based rubrics emphasized risk-taking and creativity over the final product. Some instructors believe that by completing the projects during class or making them creative and collaborative, it could lower the stakes, reduce anxiety, and make them more accessible and equitable.

By thinking about flexibility in the classroom, some instructors reflected that instead of thinking about the instructor being flexible in response to what the students were facing, ironically some instructors created a fixed set of clear and more structured material and guidance that students could access when they wanted and/ or when they could work on them. Students needed to see the clear progression of assignments so that they could pick up whenever they left off and decide what to do based on their particular situation (working in groups versus working individually, turning in an assignment that has not been completed 100%, etc.) that would let them know where they needed to be even if they had missed a class and, hopefully, ease the feeling of being overwhelmed and trying to catch up. Some instructors also mentioned that creating fixed breakout rooms and having the same group of peers to work with throughout the semester helped them to achieve the community feeling and gave them the consistency they needed to be able to rely on their group to finish their assignments and keep feeling engaged.

One of the main discussions we had with the faculty was the idea of how to balance keeping the rigor of the class while being flexible. One instructor mentioned that they shifted their model of the class where the instructor was the sole authority in the class to a shared responsibility with the whole group by having group discussions and sharing turns at talk, where everyone could contribute to the discussion rather than just listen passively to a lecture. These expectations of community knowledge build-up were established from the beginning of the semester and resulted in students being more engaged and motivated.

Finally, one faculty member mentioned that when the semester was over, and unfortunately for the students who could not complete the work that was agreed upon at the beginning of the semester, they reached out to ask for an extension on due dates. The instructor commented that they asked students to suggest a time frame to turn in the missing work and the students replied with a reasonable time to do it, letting the instructor know that what they needed was a few more days to be able to finish what they agreed to turn in. This extension in due dates was also validated by other faculty that mentioned they changed their ideal class schedule to be more in line with the "real world" calendar when thinking about what students can realistically accomplish between classes. They also talked about leaving a good part of one class (once a week or so) to talk about "nothing," and that this space would fill up quickly with unpredictable discussions that would help get a sense of community in the class instead of packing up the syllabus leaving no free space, as they used to do before.

The Center for Teaching and Learning at Columbia University recently launched a website called "Teaching Transformations: Faculty Reflections and Insights on Pandemic Practices" (https://ctl.columbia.edu/transformations/), where currently 45 faculty across disciplines in our university were invited to share their ideas, innovations and reflections on how the pandemic has transformed their teaching practices around themes such as equity and inclusion, pedagogical partnerships, course [re]design, active learning, and collaborative learning. Among some of the highlights of their reflections, one instructor mentioned how students find their class recordings useful even if they had attended class. Contrary to what the instructor thought, the class recordings did not encourage students not to show up for class. Instead, it encouraged the students to go to the recording for clarification in a particular class moment and also motivated students to contact the instructor to attend their office hours. Another instructor mentioned how the hybrid environment of their class (where some students attended in person and others joined in virtually) became a level playing field for equity in their classroom where students could come as they needed and everyone was able to get access to the class in real-time or get the recording at a later time. Another instructor mentioned that they created a detailed grading rubric from the very beginning of the semester, so students can calculate their grades at any point. What this did was give the students the flexibility and the ability to drop specific assessments and still be able to calculate their final grades. Regarding the lecture notes for the classes, several instructors mentioned that their approach was to provide as much information as they had available before class so the students could come prepared and have questions for a class discussion, others mentioned they shared their notes after the class ended so students could have a review in preparation for an exam or project. Another instructor who valued class discussion decided they would send an email to a group of students telling them they would be called to participate in the following class. This worked well for the instructor, because if for some reason they were going to be absent, they were going to be late, or they had something else that they could not prepare, they would communicate it in advance. At the same time, it did not mean that the interaction was limited to those students on the list but also allowed other students to ask questions and engage with the class.

Finally, one of the main highlights of having the Zoom environment was the luxury of bringing in more voices from a range of global regions to our particular classes. The Zoom software allowed instructors to invite wonderful guest speakers that would otherwise be very hard to bring physically to the United States. Even though videoconferencing software such as Skype was available before the pandemic, something about the pandemic opened that possibility more and diversified our field and our pedagogical guest inquiries.

CONCLUSION AND FUTURE DIRECTIONS

In this chapter, I presented the modifications in assessments made by a faculty committee in our Spanish department to create a more equitable education where students are being assessed in a way that goes in line with the expectations of an online environment. By making these modifications to our course components we made and continue making efforts to consider the context of our class, making sure we take a holistic approach by incorporating what is happening in the "real world" in line with the class expectations. By incorporating flexibility in our teaching practices, we are letting our students know that their needs and expectations have been considered when faculty design a course syllabus and assessment tasks and that their well-being matters to us.

Through the final project, students are given agency in their second language learning process when asked to make sense of and understand LL manifestations in their immediate environment. We draw on multimodal, sociocultural perspectives on language learning (Kern, 2000; New London Group, 1996)—which conceive L2 literacy development as a process of negotiating multiple discourses and semiotic signs that circulate in today's super diverse contexts—as a framework for integrating LL into our content-based Spanish as a foreign language curriculum.

The work my university has done in supporting its faculty has been invaluable. At a departmental level, we were given the resources (course releases for some and monetary stipend for others) and space to create a committee to work on such a pressing issue. At the university level, we were provided with the support of a newly created center (CEP) with professionals who were able to guide us through the moment of crisis and the space to reflect critically on our experiences (CLT) after going through a traumatic experience where our lives and the world as we knew it could come to an end. By providing strategies and spaces where faculty could receive and provide feedback on their teaching, the university created opportunities to grow through professional development, and opportunities to work with other faculty providing a sense of community. Thus, the present study supports the findings presented by Pressley and Ha (2021).

Regarding future directions, institutions need to focus on taking advantage of their local resources (i.e., technical, logistical, and human, as well as the use of city landscapes and cultural offerings) to enrich their classes and also to tap into faculty expertise when facing unexpected challenges or when trying new ideas before looking for outside professional development. Similarly, open-source materials and free access content available online are also great resources to alleviate the cost of education for students and institutions with scarce financial resources.

Focusing on the changes implemented by our department due to the COVID-19 pandemic, I hope to bring a different perspective on what could happen when an institution provides a space and resources to reflect and support each other in a moment of crisis. Finally, by bringing this perspective I do acknowledge the privilege I have and I do not want to dismiss the struggles and injustices my peers had to undergo at different institutions and different educational levels (at the primary, secondary, and university levels).

NOTE

1. My colleagues in the Department of Latin American and Iberian Cultures at Columbia and the Department of Spanish and Latin American Studies at Barnard who worked on creating the new assessments are: Leonor Pons Coll, Isaura Arce-Fernandez, Antoni Fernandez, Jesús Suárez García, Juan Pablo Jiménez-Caicedo, Lee B. Abraham, Diana Romero, Leyre Alejaldre Briel, Angelina Craig Florez, Dolores Barbazán Capeáns, Lorena García Barroso, Guadalupe Ruiz Fajardo, and myself.

REFERENCES

Blommaert, J. (2013). *Ethnography, super-diversity, and linguistic landscapes: Chronicles of complexity* (Vol. 18). Multilingual Matters.

Educators for Excellence. (2020). *Voices from the virtual classroom: A survey of America's teachers on COVID-19-related education issues*. Retrieved on June 3, 2023 from https://e4e.org/news/survey-americas-educators/voices-virtual-classroom

Gilmore, T., Krantz, J., & Ramirez, R. (1986). Action-based modes of inquiry and the host-researcher relationship. *Consultation, 5*(3), 161.

Kern, R. (2000). *Literacy and language teaching.* Oxford University Press.

Kraft, M. A., Simon, N. S., & Lyon, M. A. (2021). Sustaining a sense of success: The protective role of teacher working conditions during the COVID-19 pandemic (EdWorkingPaper: 20-279). Retrieved from Annenberg Institute at Brown University. https://doi.org/10.26300/35nj-v890

Lee, K., Fanguy, M., Lu, X. S., & Bligh, B. (2021). Student learning during COVID-19: It was not as bad as we feared. *Distance Education, 42*(1), 164–172. https://doi.org/10.1080/01587919.2020.1869529

Lozano, M. E., Jiménez-Caicedo, J. P., & Abraham, L. B. (2020). Linguistic landscape projects in language teaching: Opportunities for critical language learning beyond the classroom. In D. Malinowski, H. Maxim, & S. Dubreil (Eds.), *Language teaching in the LInguistic landscape* (pp. 17–42). Springer.

New London Group. (1996). A pedagogy of multiliteracies: Designing social futures. *Harvard Educational Review 66*(1), 60–93.

Pressley, T. (2021). Factors contributing to teacher burnout during COVID-19. *Educational Researcher, 50*(5), 325–327.

Pressley, T., & Ha, C. (2021). Teaching during a pandemic: United States teachers' self-efficacy during COVID-19. *Teaching and Teacher Education, 106*, 1–9.

Salehi, M., & Marefat, F. (2014). The effects of foreign language anxiety and test anxiety on foreign language test performance. *Theory & Practice in Language Studies, 4*(5), 931–940.

Shin, M., & Hickey, K. (2020). Needs a little TLC: Examining college students' emergency remote teaching and learning experiences during COVID-19. *Journal of Further and Higher Education, 45*(7), 973–986. https://doi.org/10.1080/0309877X.2020.1847261

Simmons, D. (2020). Why COVID-19 is our equity check. *Educational Leadership, 77*(1), 51–53.

Turan, Z., Kucuk, S., & Cilligol Karabey, S. (2022). The university students' self-regulated effort, flexibility, and satisfaction in distance education. *International Journal of Educational Technology in Higher Education, 19*, 35. https://doi.org/10.1186/s41239-022-00342-w

CHAPTER 5

NAVIGATING COMPLEXITY

Fostering Inclusive Social Environments in Bilingual Education Through Multimodal Communication

Wilder Yesid Escobar-Almeciga
Universidad El Bosque

Lorena Caviedes-Cadena
Universidad Nacional de Colombia

Fabián Benavides Jiménez
Universidad El Bosque

ABSTRACT

In 2020 and 2021, the COVID-19 pandemic prompted an abrupt shift from in-person to virtual teaching, posing challenges for English as a foreign language (EFL) classes. This chapter reflects on the experiences of an undergraduate bilingual teaching program during this transition, offering theory-based insights. The reflections explore the conceptual foundation, emphasizing the relationship between language learning and communication, and advocate for a communicative, democratic, and ethical approach to education. The implications highlight ethical considerations in classroom communication and pedagogical practices in EFL instruction, aiming for a safe, collaborative, and fair social climate conducive to learning. Keywords include bilingual education, English as a foreign language, higher education, inclusive instruction, and socio climate for learning.

Countless were the effects that the COVID-19 pandemic brought about for human interaction all over the globe. In the case of education, it forced a rapid transition from on-site and in-person interaction to virtually mediated synchronous instruction. The experience that the bilingual education undergraduate program with emphasis on the teaching of English and Spanish underwent, afforded significant reflections on the relationship among communication, the classroom's social climate, and learning. The program is offered at a private university located in the north end of Bogotá–Colombia whose origins are in the areas of medicine and health. Consequently, the university's culture is framed within the biopsychological and sociocultural paradigm, derived from that field of knowledge. It advocates for a holistic view of the person and exhorts the professionals it educates to consider the patient, student, customer, and so on, as a multidimensional, complex, and unique individual in their practices. The university also abides by the national standards for English as a foreign language (EFL), which are regulated by the Common European Framework of References for Languages (Council of Europe, 2020) and strongly enforced by the Colombian Ministry of National Education. The bilingual education undergraduate program aligns with this institutional philosophy, endeavoring the development of pedagogical, communicative, research, and socio-affective competencies. They explore these competencies by promoting an inclusive, respectful, dialogic learning social climate for students from diverse socioeconomic strata who seek a language teaching degree in English and Spanish.

As faculty, we found ourselves mobilizing staff and students of the program through the abrupt transition that the pandemic brought about. This phenomenon not only uncovered some of the most complex intricacies surrounding virtual interaction and instruction in our classes but also alerted us about some of the fallacies of technology-mediated education and the inequalities that it could potentially engender when communicative and sociocultural factors are overlooked. The unexpected experience moved us into a collective, gradual, but profound set of reflections as we reconciled our teaching and learning interactions with the technology-mediated demands of the moment. From the experience, we came to understand that English language learning does not simply require the instruction of the linguistic code. Rather, it encompasses a broader spectrum of human dimensions like the exchange of ideas, feelings, identities, emotions, backgrounds, histories, stories, etc., and it can only take place as students fully engage in the social, cultural, emotional, intellectual, and physical dynamics of the class. Within this view, we see the learning of English as benefitting from a deep commitment to each other and to communicating openly and fairly in the classroom community (Escobar-Alméciga & Brutt-Griffler, 2022; Fairclough, 2011; Gee, 2011; Hellermann, 2006; Kress, 2011).

As such, this chapter accounts for the theory-based reflections that derived from our pedagogical experience in pandemic times. It intends to collect, articulate, and deploy our most significant learnings in ways that may contribute to other pedagogical practices and to stir considerations around the relationship between communication and instruction in virtual learning environments. In more general terms, however, it also aims at grappling with the complex and reciprocal relationship between interaction and the social climate for EFL learning.

In this pursuit, we initially address the conceptual framework for learning and instruction and direct it onto the ways in which multimodal communication (e.g., use of gestures, visuals, bodily action) lies at the heart of the creation of a healthy classroom's social climate and learning (Bloome, 2001; McGee Banks & Banks, 1995; Read et al., 2015; Stuhlman & Pianta, 2009). In other words, we conceptualize learning as a social practice (Street, 2003), made possible in and through multimodal communication. Subsequently, we situate the challenges that teachers and students in our program experienced during the transition from online to virtual EFL lessons due to the COVID-19 pandemic. In doing so, we address the particular challenges that generating fluid interactions posed in the almost exclusive use of technology in the pandemic which, in turn, uncovered conditions of asymmetrical access to technology, inadequate physical spaces, and poor competencies in digital literacies in instruction and in learning. Thereafter, we present the takeaways that resulted from instruction in quarantine, and the need to instill in students and teachers a personal commitment to communicating with each other in the classroom community as paramount to achieving the type of social climate that is conducive to academic success. From our experience, we exhort educators to see communication and interaction as key elements in instructional designs to create possibilities for students to make use of their own semiotic resources to act on their own behalf. Finally, we propose a code of ethics for classroom communication in the interest of participation, collaboration, interaction, co-construction of knowledge, and more learning opportunities.

CONCEPTUAL FRAMINGS FOR EFL LEARNING AND ITS SOCIAL CLIMATE

Before exploring virtual EFL education in the quest for bilingualism, pluralism, otherness, diversity, and so on, we need first to explore our conceptualization of what learning entails. In that respect, we see learning as a social process where the objective is to become interactively competent in a subject matter and this is achieved through socialization and mediation (Ghazi et al., 2014; Vygotsky, 1978). That is, learning develops as an effect of the type of communication that learning environments and instruction therein create and promote (Escobar-Alméciga & Brutt-Griffler, 2022; Fairclough, 2011; Gee, 2011; Hellermann, 2006; Kress, 2011). From this perspective, learning happens in interactions with different voices and thus is of a social nature. People engage in communicative action through interaction by forming, transforming, negotiating, and exchanging their own cultural, historical, intellectual, emotional, cognitive, and physical (semiotic) resources with others. These processes support them in pursuit of individual and collective goals, which can be learning (Escobar-Alméciga & Brutt-Griffler, 2022; Kress, 2010).

In a complementary manner to Vygotsky's core construct of mediation, the anthropologically informed work of Hymes represented a reaction to exclusively cognitive-driven theories of language learning through his development of an ethnography of communication that explored the cultural dimensions of language use (Hymes, 1964, 1967, 1972, 1974). His work displayed a complex evolution from its origins in the 'ethnography of speaking and the structure of conversations' that focused more heavily on what the individual could do as well as on the ways in which speaking could be deconstructed into smaller structures. His work evolved into what later became the ethnography of communication. Here the focus was no longer on the individual and speaking ceased to be understood as a set of structures, and instead became a system of intricate relationships that acted and interacted in meaning-making, meaning negotiation, knowledge construction, and the formation and transformation of individual and collective identities.

Aligned with this perspective, Escobar-Alméciga (2022) and Escobar-Alméciga and Brutt-Griffler (2022) further delved into the multimodal and social nature of communication and the direct relationship it holds with language learning. They use and expand on Hymes' ethnographic take on communication, contending that meaning is distributed among many different modes, not only speech. In some cases, gestures may take on a more important role in meaning-making than the spoken mode while at other times, speech may be more salient (Callow, 2013; Jessie & Peter, 2015; Kress & Van Leeuwen, 2002).

We also draw from concepts of communication that are constructivist in nature and stem from the seminal work of Canale and Swain (1980), Cook-Gumperz et al. (1986), Habermas (1970), Hymes (1967, 1972, 1974), Schieffelin and Gilmore (1986), and Schmidt (1983). That is, sociocultural conventions are brought to bear, agreed upon, and established in the act of communication not only to negotiate meaning but also to determine the types of relationships that can and cannot be established in interaction. Accordingly, to establish positive relationships in the specific context of a school classroom, the learners' sociocultural attributes must be welcomed into the negotiation of understandings, feelings, and relationships in the sociocultural exchange therein (Ediger, 2009; Miller & Pedro, 2006; Read et al., 2015).

From this perspective, we see all available semiotic resources (including the students' L1 and sociocultural backgrounds) and communicative modes as having a central role in classroom interaction and hence, in learning in two main ways: (a) they offer additional opportunities for students to partake of class dynamics while welcoming diverse ways of (inter) acting, (inter) being, (inter) feeling, (inter) knowing, and (inter) representing. They also (2) promote a commitment to communicating with others in diversified ways, which is paramount to learning (Aukerman et al., 2017; Escobar-Alméciga, 2022; Escobar-Alméciga & Brutt-Griffler, 2022). In embracing these full ranges of meaning-making resources, education practices begin to offer a more ample repertoire of possibilities for students to bring in their particularities, backgrounds and cosmogonies. In so doing, they value everyone in their differences and similarities and provide opportunities for full participation, collaboration, interaction, and production and hence, for learning while bringing diverse students out of the invisibility that mainstream education often engenders (Correa et al., 2014; Escobar-Alméciga & Gómez Lobaton, 2010; Soler & Pardo, 2007).

To make matters worse, interactions in pandemic times suffered the most dramatic change of social distancing, posing complications in most areas of human life and accelerating the spread of technology-mediated interactions. While technology-mediated communication facilitated the job in many business-related endeavors, in education, it reduced the possibilities for nurturing a commitment to students' communicative action. communicating with others in synchronous class sessions. Interactions in student communication were mediated by cold, mechanical, distant, and technological resources that obstructed most qualities of human communication. One example was evidenced in the pedagogy-related courses of the program. While in face-to face sessions, students were able to resort to their gazes, body orientation, proxemics, and smiles to invite, accept, reject, or agree to interactions with others in the classroom. However, online sessions made those semiotic resources unavailable for students and for teachers. Synchronous class sessions were mediated by video conferencing tools where students proved hesitant to turn their cameras on, to speak freely and fluidly, and to address other students in the class. These circumstances restricted the degree to which interactions could be multidirectional and they posed serious challenges to manage silences and adhere to the time schedules for class activities. Additionally, a commitment to communicating assertively and unswervingly with each other in the class was more difficult to instill in students in online environments and in pursuit of a welcoming social climate. Thus, communicative (learning) environments that were migrated to spaces where social exchange and social action had significant restrictions in terms of the type of semiotic resources and communicative modes that could be formed, transformed, and used in meaning negotiation.

To various degrees, the social climate for learning is always charged with powerful social and affective undercurrents, which in turn, determine the type of learning that takes place and the levels of student success (Ambrose et al., 2010; Freiberg, 2005; Haynes et al., 1997; Hoffman et al., 2009). Rather than being static, the social and emotional dynamics of the class are fluid and can be set off by several aspects. Such aspects vary from logistical decisions like class sizes, seating arrangements, class transitions, and so on to more abstract matters like communication, the type of interactions being promoted, the individual as well as the social positioning of the classroom members, and other similar matters (Caviedes, 2015; Caviedes et al., 2016; Escobar-Alméciga, 2022; Stuhlman & Pianta, 2009). Just like environmental climate, classes require permanent monitoring and ongoing intervention in the quest for safe, healthy, and edifying social climates, which are founded upon a commitment to communicating with others in the quest for positive human relations of cooperation, solidarity, and community building (Ali & Siddiqui, 2016; Ediger, 2009; Miller & Pedro, 2006; Read et al., 2015; Wasik, 2008).

Put differently, students create and accumulate subjective knowledge that shapes their behaviors, emotions, thoughts, relations, and ways of acting and interacting in social exchange. Through time and interaction, such exchange institutes the set of sociocultural conventions that will be recognized as the group's own—that is, particular ways of speaking, envisioning reality, and relating to their physical and social surroundings—figured worlds (Fairclough, 2011). In turn, this establishes membership that generates feelings of belonging and commitment towards others in the group. This sense of affiliation can create a classroom community where the students' sociocultural backgrounds and their unique personality traits are embraced in the act of communication and learning (Bloome, 2001; Canale & Swain, 1980; Cook-Gumperz et al., 1986; Escobar-Alméciga & Brutt-Griffler, 2022; Habermas, 1970; Hymes, 1964, 1967, 1972, 1974; Schieffelin

& Gilmore, 1986; Schmidt, 1983). Consequently, this encourages students to claim ownership over what happens in the classroom and empowers them to act as agents of change to support their collective interests in the varied learning environments that they may inhabit (Bloome, 2001; McGee Banks & Banks, 1995; Read et al., 2015; Stuhlman & Pianta, 2009).

As such, Arter (1987) recommends a close examination of four dimensions when assessing the quality of the learning climate. The first dimension pertains to the nature and quality of the relationships established. To assess this aspect, we investigate the ways in which students and teachers communicate with each other, their feelings toward one another, and the relationships that are made possible in the classroom. This can be observed through the types of interactions—whether students are readily willing to help others, or whether their interactions are tainted with hostility or competitiveness. The second dimension refers to personal development. For teachers, this dimension comprises the opportunities afforded to them to improve their instructional approach and the degree to which they are supported in the process. For students, this concerns the possibility of emotional and intellectual growth that the classroom dynamics allow. Examining this dimension requires close attention to how interactions make students feel, the level of comfort with which students experience classroom dynamics, and the extent to which such experiences allow them to advance in their intellectual, emotional, and social development. The third dimension is called system maintenance and change, and it refers to the extent to which expectations are clear. This dimension considers whether students are aware of the types of behaviors and interactions that are acceptable and valued in the classroom and whether such behaviors and interactions are also modeled by others. It also concerns the ability to make instructional adjustments as situations arise. A final dimension, called physical environment, alludes to the extent to which the physical features of the classroom—seating arrangements, classroom decorations and so on—or the layout of a virtual space are conducive to creating a pleasant and productive work atmosphere.

Since virtual learning environments have limitations for interaction, a commitment toward communication needs to be instilled in students to experience the type of investment that results in cooperation among them and that facilitates learning opportunities as a social practice (Stuhlman & Pianta, 2009). In other words, the design of education programs often envisions the population they intend to serve as a homogenous group of students usually with the characteristics of the dominant group (De Sousa Santos, 2021; Walsh, 2010). Hence, "diversity" is often overlooked or misconceived as an issue, which needs to be mitigated by assimilating non-mainstream students into mainstream social norms. This assimilation denies students the opportunity to engage in unexpected, diversified, and atypical interactions that are often misinterpreted and disregarded in instruction (McGee Banks & Banks, 1995; Miller & Pedro, 2006; Read et al., 2015). These reflections on the relationship between communication and learning are based on the following experiences in the Bilingual-Teaching Program as a result of the accelerated transition and the new conditions for education.

RECOGNIZING THE ROLE OF INTERACTION IN THE CONSTRUCTION OF THE EFL SOCIAL CLIMATE

When the COVID-19 pandemic emerged, lockdowns began to reduce possibilities for class interaction, and even more drastically, for those students from low-income families who did not have the financial and technological resources or the access to the type of infrastructure that supported the Internet and the educational interphases therein. For instance, the lack of computers at students' homes forced learning and teaching processes to be mediated by personal cell phones at best, and asynchronous educational packages at worst. Before the pandemic, the social gap between those who had the resource and those who did not was noticeable to a degree. However, the transformation that interactions between student and teacher and among students had to suffer in such conditions of isolation and social distancing made it ever more evident in educational contexts.

In Colombia only 52,7% of the population has regular access to the Internet (Departamento Administrativo Nacional de Estadística, 2018). Hence, it would probably go without saying that virtual education in the different school levels and across the national territory has been inaccessible to a significant number of students regardless of the conditions that COVID-19 brought about. That is, the pandemic only made such a gap more evident. The specific case of EFL online learning in our program was not the exception. For students to develop communicative competence in a foreign language, they needed to use the language in social interactions. However, access to technological devices and to the Internet for learning and instruction was not evenly available, which meant that not everyone had access to the classes that were strategically migrated to virtual environments (Fořtová et al., 2021; García Botero et al., 2021; Izquierdo et al., 2021). Beyond the disproportionate distribution of technological resources, the pandemic introduced additional challenges when our program attempted to create online educational spaces extrapolated onto students' homes. For example, in the university classrooms, students had a regulated learning environment with lighting, seating furniture, Wi-Fi access, and noise-reduced conditions. At the students' homes, learners were left with the responsibility of reconciling their house infrastructure, disruptive family interactions, lack of Internet access and connectivity with their EFL learning demands.

In addition to the adverse conditions that migrating school to the students' homes posed for learning and instruction, social interactions also suffered a significant metamorphosis. In face-to-face classroom encounters, students had the possibility to initiate their interactions with friendly conventions like handshakes, smiles, stories, gazes, proxemics, physical contact, compliments, and conversations, whereas once students moved into the virtual environments, interactions were mediated by conferencing tools that restricted the possibilities to use these semiotic resources and modes for interaction. Thus, class sessions no longer began with the mingling of students and their socio-affective demonstrations. In addition, students were more hesitant to speak out of turn or address their classmates in class conversations. Gazes, smiles, and face expressions were limited to the extent to which the students were willing to turn on their devices. However, students were very hesitant to activate their cameras, microphones, and other mediating resources for class activities, generating breakdowns in class interaction (Alawamleh et al., 2022).

Rather than experiencing an interactive environment where students were discursively empowered to relate to contents and others, interaction became bidirectional between teacher and students and conversations among students were ever more difficult to promote. Consequently, student–teacher–student exchanges became the norm. In most cases, adapting to the new circumstances and resorting to alternative digital tools turned communication stale and constrained. As an effect, students' participation and commitment to the learning process lagged and their willingness to communicate decreased. In this case, technological advances proved inadequate in mediating the type of communication that usually took place during in-person teaching and learning because, in these virtual spaces, communication was enacted awkwardly through monosyllabic responses, uniformed turn-taking, and prolonged speech pauses. Conversations were also interrupted by microphone and camera malfunctions, reducing class interaction to writing on the chat at best and complete student absence at worst.

The most salient aftermath of the above-mentioned challenges became evident upon the abrupt transition from virtual classes back to in-person classes after the pandemic. We observed how students who enrolled in the program during the quarantine exhibited difficulties when class activities demanded collective work or public speaking. More precisely, in classes that used English as a medium of instruction, interactions were awkward and strenuous due to the lack of face-to-face conversations that people had during such a time. Students were uncomfortable interacting with others in the class: insecurities about their English proficiency, speaking in front of an audience, and mere social contact skyrocketed in socialization. The aforementioned issues of the virtual environment made the sessions less conducive to an amicable social climate for learners to meet, relate, coexist, and learn. For teachers, this made it difficult to instill in students a shared commitment to communicate with each other and to invest in their social relations, celebrating their differences and likenesses (otherness) in their communicative action as mediated by virtual tools (Crozier et al., 2016).

In times of the pandemic, teachers and students experienced communication that lacked possibilities for interaction, (full) participation, cooperation, and the use of sociocultural and emotional resources in virtual spaces. The role of the teacher as a communicative agent was also restrained by the shortcomings that the virtual environments presented as the means of communicating. The social climate therein was cold, distant, awkward, and inadequate for the collective construction of knowledge. Such particularities stirred our interest in inquiring and understanding the reciprocities among communication, instruction, and learning in the bilingual teaching program. We sought to recognize and acknowledge the different characteristics, roles, and communicative actions that each stakeholder–institution, teachers, students, and the like—had or could potentially exert in the processes of teaching and learning.

ENDEAVORING A LEARNING-CONDUCIVE SOCIAL CLIMATE FOR THE PANDEMIC AFTERMATH

The social phenomenon described above guided us into thinking about teaching methods that would respond to such challenges, in terms of communication, interaction, (full) participation, and collaboration. Even though communicative approaches to teaching were at the heart of the program long before the event, the arrival of a rough transition left teachers and students with little or no time to rethink and reconstruct their teaching and learning of social behaviors within their emergent virtual environments, reducing the pursuit of a learning-conducive social climate.

The pedagogical culture at the heart of our commitment to the program considered the necessary characteristics for classroom communication to become conducive to learning. We also explored how instructional designs could foster deep considerations for classroom communication. With a critical approach and interest in local world views, we promoted different and collective ways of knowing, struggling over knowledge, participating, and accounting for the knowledge constructed (De Sousa Santos, 2009).

More precisely and directly related to the bilingual-teaching program, teachers met in focal groups to reflect upon three main issues: (a) the role of communication inside the program and in their courses; (b) ways in which the courses could be deployed in the interest of communication, participation, and plurality creating a visual flow chart and explaining the logic behind it; and (c) ways of creating learning climates that fostered students' interaction in the transition from the virtually mediated spaces used in pandemic times to face-to-face on-sight instruction. With this in mind, there were five meetings, distributed as shown in Table 5.1.

After the sessions, we created an additional opportunity for all the program faculty with their own particular backgrounds and worldviews to meet. There, they recapitulated on the activities that aimed to develop an interactive teaching-learning culture which sought to (a) accept every member of the group as unique and valuable in the social construction of the class; (b) promote collective dialogue among teachers and students valuing and welcoming diverse perspectives, backgrounds, histories, stories, identities and the like; (c) frame our program culture within the polyphonies of their stakeholders and the broader established communities of practice; and (d) reduce the tendency of dealing with knowledge in the fragmentation of disciplines, which does not allow us to conceive education problems in a global, holistic, and yet, fundamental manner (Morin, 2011).

As a result, this collective work yielded four significant considerations that could be incorporated into curricular design to achieve a cohesive pedagogical proposal. First, we consider flexibility as the key to offering diverse, equal, and ample opportunities for students to participate while raising awareness about the power of communicative action and the way this power can be used to foster or inhibit learning. Second, we consider the

TABLE 5.1 Actions Within the Pedagogical Proposal of the Bilingual-Teaching Program

Meeting	Actions	Outcomes
1	The program faculty met in small groups to socialize the current syllabi and received feedback from colleagues.	Suggestions on syllabi for the improvement of each course.
2	Each professor worked on the flow chart of the course and an explanation behind it. They also applied improvements on the syllabi in terms of establishing objectives and learning outcomes, as well as in their internal and articulated design conducive to communication and learning.	Updated syllabi in terms of objectives and learning outcomes in pursuit of co-constructed communicative-learning environments. Course flowchart.
3	In small groups, professors shared the changes in the syllabi of the courses they taught to find common grounds and logic sequencing of the subject courses within the broader program.	Presentation of the syllabi and articulation with the other subject courses. Presentation of the flowchart.
4	Final amendments in the micro and the macro structures of the subject courses and their syllabi and the socialization of the resulting products with the entire group of professors.	Updated syllabi and finalized flowchart of the course.
5	Submission of updated syllabi and flowchart.	Updated syllabi and flowchart.

Note: Own elaboration

importance of design course-sequencing—*the "who does what? when? how?"* in the teaching and learning processes—so that they are logically articulated, scaffolded, and cohesive. A third aspect refers to the extent to which each subject course was framed within the philosophy of the institution. A final aspect refers to the importance of co-constructed spaces for professors to imagine their classes as democratic, ethical and communicative scenarios in which professors and students come together to build their social worlds in collaboration, sharing rights, and responsibilities while nurturing a commitment towards others and toward their own learning.

When the program faculty debriefed about these newly introduced processes, they expressed the view that learning is a result of communication and, thus, course-designs must deeply contemplate the possibilities it would afford the students for interaction, (full) participation, collaboration, communication, and production. They recognized that bringing their instructional designs and their course proposals into a dialogue with their colleagues provided them with the big picture. They saw the collective work as opening a window of opportunity for the cohesive articulation of the program where all subject areas would be taught capitalizing on these common grounds and endeavor common objectives. They were particularly key in creating respectful, appreciative, safe, and edifying social learning climates. These learning climates involved viewing students holistically, considering all their human dimensions. The aim was to create an environment where students felt comfortable communicating their ideas, performing their identities, and exchanging their cultures and knowledge in alignment with the institutional philosophy. In general, they developed a new appreciation for instilling a dialogic classroom culture where students grappled with knowledge, identities, and cultures ethically and respectfully valuing differences and likenesses equally.

Understanding the COVID-19 pandemic as an event that abruptly changed the ways people communicated with each other translates directly into the transformation of their ways of (inter)being, (inter)acting (inter) feeling, (inter) knowing, and (inter) representing. Moreover, understanding the changes caused by the pandemic also highlights the ways of learning and the challenges it presented for instruction. As such, our reflections in this section allude to the ways in which teachers progressively became active agents in the designs of social and emotional scenarios, allowing students to learn through multimodal interaction and become committed to reciprocal communication in virtual environments. More precisely, this experience accounts for the way interactions were transformed and migrated to technology-mediated spaces, and the new ways in which the students related personally, interpersonally, and cognitively in their virtual and social environments. This propelled the rethinking of learning and instruction as students migrated to digital worlds and as interaction was breached, but somehow also distanced by technology.

ETHICS IN CLASSROOM COMMUNICATION FOR BILINGUALISM

The processes of teaching and learning are intricately interwoven within broader contextual framings and social situations. Consequently, communication is at the heart of pedagogy and learning and has the potential to create social climates that either foster or inhibit interaction, (full)participation, and collaboration, as well as the collective construction of meaning, social relations, and knowledge. The experience at the Bilingual Teaching Program offered us three overarching takeaways concerning a healthy and learning-conducive social climate and the way teachers could promote it.

First, the transformation from traditional classroom dynamics into cooperative classroom communities requires a profound commitment of each member (students and teacher) to class communication where everyone is invested in class conversations and seeks opportunities to interact and to construct a welcoming social climate. That is to say, teachers are left with the charge of designing spaces that, first, empowers students to bring in their unique ways of (inter) acting, (inter) being (inter) knowing, (inter) feeling, and (inter) representing, and, secondly, develops a sense of commitment to listening to, grappling with, and taking up their classmates' ideas, feelings, thoughts, and so on. For such a pursuit, it becomes paramount to instill in students a type of sensitivity that allows them to become aware and accepting of the likenesses and differences that we all bring into classroom interaction. Students need to come to the realization that while it is important to exert communicative action to act on one's own behalf, this always influences others whether it be positive or negative. One's communicative action can strengthen relationships, edify sentiments, mediate meaning negotiation, and be conducive to learning, or it can undermine, diminish, and marginalize others (Arter, 1987; Bloome, 2001; Escobar-Alméciga, 2013; Escobar-Alméciga et al., 2013; Gumperz, 1986; Hall et al., 2004; Hellermann, 2006; Jennings & Greenberg, 2009; Moll et al., 2001; Wasik, 2008). The learning process is filled with adverse situations for learners, particularly when the classroom culture is based upon competitiveness, predisposition, and animosity. This affects and diminishes assertive communication and meaningful participation among students. To avoid such a classroom culture, teachers need to uphold solidarity in the classroom by promoting a learning environment where students readily come in to support the processes of others while feeling that they may very well become recipients of collaboration, acceptance, and kindness when they face difficulties in their own processes.

Second, teachers could potentially incite inequalities in language education when they create disproportionate possibilities for students to access social goods in class. For instance, the opportunities that students have to form, transform, and make use of their own semiotic resources may or may not encourage them to act according to their benefit and partake of the problem-solving dynamics of the collective interactions of the class (Escobar-Alméciga, 2020; Escobar-Alméciga & Brutt-Griffler, 2022; Kress, 2010). In that sense, teachers have the challenge of discerning, interpreting, thinking, rethinking, and configuring the type of communication that promotes fair opportunities for students to exert communicative action, participate, and learn. In such a light, "teaching" does not only entail the delivery of information. Rather, "teaching" becomes the act by which the teacher designs and deploys communicative opportunities for students to be able to resort to their own semiotic resources, encouraging students to act and interact in the quest for learning.

Third, a common teaching pitfall has to do with believing that the teacher should always be at the center of class interaction and that students should answer what the teacher has come to decide is the *right* answer. This constrains the extent to which students can exert agency in the process. Instead, teachers could acknowledge that students are not empty vessels and that they have a cultural, emotional, historical, intellectual, and social background that shapes the way in which they grapple with content, concepts, and ideas. This has a profound effect on the way teachers conceive concepts like assessment, feedback, and evaluation. In such a light, they no longer see those concepts as evidence of learning, but as opportunities for building off from what the students have previously constructed while recognizing and valuing their background-derived contributions to an emerging social process. Thus, rather than being overly concerned about having students respond or behave in a desired manner, teachers need to develop an interpretative competence that allows them to see beyond the literal, concrete, and expected content that the student produces. In so doing, teachers can potentially recognize the "right" *in* the "wrong"—those distant associations with some logic that students draw on and are often difficult to discern.

REFERENCES

Alawamleh, M., Al-Twait, L. M., & Al-Saht, G. R. (2022). The effect of online learning on communication between instructors and students during Covid-19 pandemic. *Asian Education and Development Studies, 11*(2), 380–400. https://doi.org/10.1108/AEDS-06-2020-0131

Ali, Z. Z., & Siddiqui, M. (2016). School climate: Learning environment as a predictor of a student's academic achievement. *Journal of Research & Reflections in Education, 10*(1), 104–115. https://www.prdb.pk/article/school-climate-learning-environment-as-a-predictor-of-stude-2997

Ambrose, S. A., Bridges, M. W., DiPietro, M., Lovett, M. C., & Norman, M. K. (2010). *How learning works: Seven research-based principles for smart teaching.* Wiley.

Arter, J. A. (1987). *Assessing school and classroom climate. A consumer's guide* (ERIC Document Reproduction Services No. ED295301). Northwest Regional Educational Lab. https://files.eric.ed.gov/fulltext/ED295301.pdf

Aukerman, M., Moore Johnson, E., & Chambers Schuldt, L. (2017). Reciprocity of student and teacher discourse practices in monologically and dialogically organized text discussion. *Journal of Language & Literacy Education, 13*(2), 1–52. http://jolle.coe.uga.edu/wp-content/uploads/2017/11/Aukerman_JoLLE2017.pdf

Bloome, D. (2001). Building literacy and the classroom community. *Theory Into Practice, 25*(2), 71–76. https://doi.org/10.1080/00405848609543203

Callow, J. (2013). *The shape of text to come.* Primary English Teaching Association Australia. http://static.booktopia.com.au/pdf/9781875622870-1.pdf

Canale, M., & Swain, M. (1980). Theoretical bases of communicative approaches to second language teaching and testing. *Applied linguistics, 1*(1), 1–47. https://doi.org/10.1093/applin/I.1.1

Caviedes, L. (2015). From underdogs to important speakers: Unveiling language learning identities through peer-approval discourses. In W. Escobar (Ed.), *Análisis del discurso aplicado a la enseñanza del inglés en contextos colombianos: teoría y métodos.* http://hdl.handle.net/20.500.12495/2821.

Caviedes L., Meza A., & Rodríguez I. (2016). Collaborative work and language learners' identities when editing academic texts. *HOW Journal, 23*(2), 58–74. https://doi.org/10.19183/how.23.2.267

Cook-Gumperz, J., Corsaro, W., & Streeck, J. (1986). *Children's worlds and children's language.* De Gruyter Mouton. https://doi.org/10.1515/9783110864212

Correa, D., Usma, J., & Montoya, J. C. (2014). El Programa Nacional de Bilingüismo: Un estudio exploratorio en el Departamento de Antioquia, Colombia. *Íkala, revidepartamentosta de lenguaje y cultura, 19*(1), 101–116.

Council of Europe. (2020). *Common European framework of reference for languages: Learning, teaching, assessment* (Companion volume). Council of Europe Publishing. www.coe.int/lang-cefr

Crozier, G., Burke, P. J., & Archer, L. (2016). Peer relations in higher education: Raced, classed and gendered constructions and othering. *Whiteness and Education, 1*(1), 39–53. https://doi.org/10.1080/23793406.2016.1164746

Departamento Administrativo Nacional de Estadística. (2018). *Indicadores básicos de tenencia y uso de tecnologías de la información y comunicación*—TIC en hogares y personas de 5 y más años de edad. Boletín Técnico. https://www.dane.gov.co/files/investigaciones/boletines/tic/bol_tic_hogares_2018.pdf

De Sousa Santos, B. (2009). A non-occidentalist west? Learned ignorance and ecology of knowledge. *Theory, Culture, & Society, 26*(7–8), 103–125. https://doi.org/10.1177/0263276409348079

De Sousa Santos, B. (2021). *Descolonizar la Universidad: El desafío de la justicia cognitiva global.* Clacso.

Ediger, M. (2009). Seven criteria for an effective classroom environment. *College Student Journal, 43*(4), 1370–1373. https://link.gale.com/apps/doc/A21751 1798/AONE?u=gauniv&sid=googleScholar&xid=b48aefa9

Escobar-Alméciga, W. Y. (2013). Identity-forming discourses: A critical discourse analysis on policy making processes concerning English language teaching in Colombia. *Profile: Issues in Teachers' Professional Development, 15*(1), 45–60. https://revistas.unal.edu.co/index.php/profile/article/view/37861

Escobar-Alméciga, W. Y. (2020). *Ethnography of multimodal communication in an English-medium university-level classroom: A social semiotic perspective on learning* [Unpublished doctoral dissertation]. State University of New York at Buffalo.

Escobar-Alméciga, W. Y. (2022). Framing English as a medium of instruction within the Iberian-American Spanish-speaking Education contexts. *Profile: Issues in Teachers' Professional Development, 24*(1), 211–225. https://doi.org/10.15446/profile.v24n1.93434

Escobar-Alméciga, W., & Brutt-Griffler, J. (2022). Multimodal communication in an early childhood bilingual education setting: A social semiotic interaction analysis. *Íkala Revista de Lenguaje y Cultura, 27*(1), 85–106. https://doi.org/10.17533/udea.ikala.v27n1a05

Escobar-Alméciga, W. Y., Evans, R., Rodríguez Guerra, J. L., Guzmán, H. R., Mancera López, L. J., Betancur Lozano, K. L., Quevedo Gómez, Y. C. P. Pérez, R. A. Montenegro, N., Torres, C. V., & Molina, J. K. (2013). *Investigación social aplicada a la enseñanza del inglés en contextos colombianos: Teoría y métodos*. En Universidad El Bosque eBooks. https://repositorio.unbosque.edu.co/handle/20.500.12495/2819

Escobar-Alméciga, W. Y., & Gómez Lobatón, J. C. (2010). Silenced fighters: Identity, language and thought of the Nasa people in bilingual contexts of Colombia. *Profile: Issues in Teachers' Professional Development, 12*(1), 125–140. http://www.scielo.org.co/scielo.php?script=sci_arttext&pid=S1657-07902010000100009

Fairclough, N. (2011). Semiotic aspects of social transformation and learning. In R. Rogers (Ed.), *An introduction to critical discourse analysis in education* (pp. 147–155). Routledge.

Fořtová, N., Sedláčková, J., & Tůma, F. (2021). And my screen wouldn't share: Student-teachers' perceptions of ICT in online teaching practice and online Ttaching. *Íkala, Revista De Lenguaje Y Cultura, 26*(3), 513–529. https://doi.org/10.17533/udea.ikala.v26n3a03

Freiberg, H. J. (2005). *School climate: Measuring, improving, and sustaining healthy learning environments*. Falmer Press.

García Botero, J., García Botero, G., & Botero Restrepo, M. A. (2021). FL pre-service teachers' psychosocial aspects and educational conditions during the COVID-19 pandemic lockdown. *Íkala, Revista De Lenguaje Y Cultura, 26*(3), 553–569. https://doi.org/10.17533/udea.ikala.v26n3a05

Gee, J. P. (2011). Discourse analysis: What makes it critical. In R. Rogers (Ed.), *An introduction to critical discourse analysis in education* (pp. 19–50). Routledge.

Ghazi, S. R., Khan, U. A., Shahzada, G., & Ullah, K. (2014). Formal operational stage of Piaget's cognitive development theory: An implication in learning mathematics. *Journal of Educational Research, 17*(2), 71–84.

Gumperz, J. C. (Ed.). (1986). *The social construction of literacy*. Cambridge University Press.

Habermas, J. (1970). Towards a theory of communicative competence. *Inquiry, 13*(1–4), 360–375. https://doi.org/10.1080/00201747008601597

Hall, J. K., Vitanova, G., & Marchenkova, L. A. (Eds.). (2004). *Dialogue with Bakhtin on second and foreign language learning: New perspectives*. Routledge.

Haynes, N. M., Emmons, C., & Ben-Avie, M. (1997). School climate as a factor in student adjustment and achievement. *Journal of Educational and Psychological Consultation, 8*(3), 321–329. https://doi.org/10.1207/s1532768xjepc0803_4

Hellermann, J. (2006). Classroom interactive practices for developing L2 literacy: A microethnographic study of two beginning adult learners of English. *Applied Linguistics, 27*(3), 377–404. https://doi.org/10.1093/applin/ami052

Hoffman, L. L., Hutchinson, C. J., & Reiss, E. (2009). On improving school climate: Reducing reliance on rewards and punishment. *International Journal of Whole Schooling, 5*(1), 13–24. https://files.eric.ed.gov/fulltext/EJ834298.pdf

Hymes, D. (1964). 'Introduction: Towards ethnographies of communication. *American Anthropologist, 66*(6), 1–35.

Hymes, D. (1967). Models of the interaction of language and social setting. *Journal of Social Issues, 23*(2), 8–28.

Hymes, D. (1972). On communicative competence. In J. Pride & A. Holmes (Eds.), *Sociolinguistics* (pp. 269–293). Penguin.

Hymes, D. (1974). *Foundations in sociolinguistics: An ethnographic perspective.* University of Pennsylvania.

Izquierdo, J., Sandoval Caraveo, M. d.-C., De la Cruz Villegas, V., & Zapata Díaz, R. (2021). University language instructors' preparedness for technology-mediated instruction and burnout during the COVID-19 pandemic. *Íkala, Revista De Lenguaje Y Cultura, 26*(3), 661–695. https://doi.org/10.17533/udea.ikala.v26n3a11

Jennings, P. A., & Greenberg, M. T. (2009). The prosocial classroom: Teacher social and emotional competence in relation to student and classroom outcomes. *Review of Educational Research, 79*(1), 491–525. https://doi.org/10.3102/0034654308325693

Jessie, N. W. Q., & Peter, T. C. S. (2015). Every teacher, a caring educator: A multimodal discourse analysis of a teacher recruitment video in Singapore. *Multimodal Communication, 4*(1), 15–29. https://doi.org/10.1515/mc-2015-0003

Kress, G. (2010). *Multimodality: A social semiotic approach to contemporary communication.* Routledge.

Kress, G. (2011). Discourse analysis and education: A multimodal social semiotic approach. In R. Rogers (Ed.), *An introduction to critical discourse analysis in education* (pp. 205–226). Routledge.

Kress, G., & Van Leeuwen, T. (2002). Colour as a semiotic mode: Notes for a grammar of colour. *Visual Communication, 1*(3), 343–368. https://doi.org/10.1177/147035720200100306

McGee Banks, C. A., & Banks, J. A. (1995). Equity pedagogy: An essential component of multicultural education. *Theory into practice, 34*(3), 152–158. https://www.jstor.org/stable/1476634

Miller, R., & Pedro, J. (2006). Creating respectful classroom environments. *Early Childhood Education Journal, 33*(5), 293–299. https://doi.org/10.1007/s10643-006-0091-1

Moll, L. C., Sáez, R., & Dworin, J. (2001). Exploring biliteracy: Two student case examples of writing as a social practice. *Elementary School Journal, 101*(4), 435–449. http://www.jstor.org/stable/1002131

Morin, E. (2011). *La Vía. Para el futuro de la humanidad.* Grupo Planeta Spain.

Read, K., Aldridge, J., Ala'i, K., Fraser, B., & Fozdar, F. (2015). Creating a climate in which students can flourish: A whole school intercultural approach. *International Journal of Whole Schooling, 11*(2), 29–44. https://files.eric.ed.gov/fulltext/EJ1074176.pdf

Schieffelin, B. B., & Gilmore, P. (1986). *The acquisition of literacy: Ethnographic perspectives*. Ablex.

Schmidt, R. (1983). Interaction, acculturation and the acquisition of communicative competence. In N. Wolfson & E. Judd (Eds.), *Sociolinguistics and second language acquisition* (pp. 137–174). Newbury House.

Soler, S., & Pardo, N. (2007). Discurso y racismo en Colombia: Cinco siglos de invisibilidad y exclusión. In T. A. van Dijk (Ed.), *Racismo y discurso en América Latina* (pp. 181–228). Gedisa.

Street, B. (2003). What's "new" in new literacy studies? Critical approaches to literacy in theory and practice. *Current Issues in Comparative Education, 5*(2), 77–91.

Stuhlman, M. W., & Pianta, R. C. (2009). Profiles of educational quality in first grade. *The Elementary School Journal, 109*(4), 323–342. https://doi.org/10.1086/593936

Vygotsky, L. S. (1978). *Mind in society: The development of higher psychological process*. Harvard University Press.

Walsh, C. (2010). Interculturalidad crítica y educación intercultural. *Construyendo interculturalidad crítica, 75*(96), 167–181.

Wasik, B. (2008). When fewer is more: Small groups in early childhood classrooms. *Early Childhood Education Journal, 35*(6), 515–521. https://doi.org/10.1007/s10643-008-0245-4

CHAPTER 6

COMPARING ELEMENTARY SCHOOL TEACHERS' CULTURALLY RESPONSIVE PRACTICES IN CHINA AND THE UNITED STATES DURING AND BEYOND THE COVID-19 PANDEMIC

Alicia R. Thompson
Virginia Commonwealth University

Yaoying Xu
Virginia Commonwealth University

ABSTRACT

Effective teaching has long been crucial for student achievement, both before and during the pandemic. Worldwide, there are high expectations for teacher and student performance, emphasizing culturally responsive pedagogy to address individual and systemic learning gaps. This chapter explores the cultural responsiveness of elementary school teachers in China and the United States using video-cued ethnography and culture circles. The authors compare approaches in the two global contexts and recommend: (a) implementing school-based culture circles to encourage questioning of current realities and leverage existing knowledge; (b) fostering family and community partnerships; and (c) addressing gaps in evidence-based practices. While the qualitative study's findings are not generalizable, they suggest the importance of increasing teachers' knowledge of multicultural education and culturally responsive teaching to mitigate bias, enhance connection with students and families of diverse backgrounds, and reflect on the curriculum.

Effective teaching is one of the most important factors in student achievement. Throughout the world, there are high expectations for both teacher and student performance, and in particular, the importance of students developing 21st-century skills to enhance their ability to problem solve, think creatively, and collaborate on challenges that are yet to be determined. COVID-19 created additional unexpected challenges as well as opportunities for developing innovation approaches to effective teaching and learning. One opportunity as a result of the COVID pandemic is developing multiple ways to identify and access culturally responsive supports and resources to ensure effective learning across contexts. Along with these new expectations, teachers and students need to understand and navigate the demographic and cultural shifts occurring around the world and within their communities, including the ethnic, linguistic, and socioeconomic diversity of the population.

Currently, over half of the world's population lives in cities, up from 30% in 1950. As the shift from agriculture to industrialization continues, the percentage is projected to increase to 60% by 2030 (United Nations, 2019). Increased urbanization is reflective of both rural-to-urban migration and the transformation of rural areas into cities. All regions will become more urbanized, and most will see declines in their rural populations. This will be especially true for less developed countries (Hayutin, 2007). In addition, many national boundaries have become more relaxed and fluid. This is in part because technology has shortened distances and made migration easier (Hayutin, 2007). Fertility and longevity rates also have an impact on the population. National and international migration patterns, along with changing age structures, are transforming the demographic makeup of each nation and will create opportunities and challenges.

Over the next century, addressing services for these shifts will be critical as leaders consider how to redesign social, economic, and political institutions. Schools will play a critical role in this transition as they will need to prepare students for the new landscape. Developing a critical mass of educational stakeholders who are passionate, committed, and prepared to lead efforts to eliminate disparities based on ethnic, linguistic, religious, and socioeconomic status will be essential to building healthy communities (Banks & McGee Banks, 2004, 2012; Cole, 2008).

Teacher preparation programs, where most new teachers get their training, traditionally provide content and opportunities for teacher candidates to practice on a body of knowledge about classroom management that is culturally responsive. There is, however, little consensus about which facets of classroom management should be taught and practiced. Linda Darling-Hammond (2006), one of the field's intellectual leaders, argues teachers should learn to "manage many kinds of learning and teaching, through effective means of organizing and presenting information, managing discussions, organizing cooperative learning strategies, and supporting individual and group inquiry" (p. 4). Teachers have consistently identified the need for additional on-site training in classroom management to further develop skills not adequately addressed in preservice programs (Kwok, 2021; Reinke et al., 2011; Tillery et al., 2010). Teachers reported consulting with a colleague or mentor to be a preferred method for learning new classroom management strategies (Clunies-Ross et al., 2008; Kwok, 2021; Tillery et al., 2010). Merrett and Wheldall (1993) found that 82% of teachers developed classroom management skills by collaborating with peers to reflect on challenges and formulate solutions. Researchers have recommended that additional themes that foster and promote active student participation and engagement, as well as opportunities for teachers to receive feedback and reflect on practices, are needed overall (Clunies-Ross et al., 2008; Kwok, 2021; Merrett & Wheldall, 1993; Tillery et al., 2010). As globalization has become more prevalent, there is a strong need to recognize the challenges posed by diversity and examine the effectiveness of teachers' cultural competency and reflective practices. Utilizing comparative research across countries is certainly evident in areas like student achievement, curriculum, and evaluation. However, little work has been done to examine the effectiveness of teacher education through the lens of adaptive expertise within the contexts of multicultural education and culturally responsive teaching.

PURPOSE

The purpose of this chapter is to demonstrate a framework that can inform, guide, expand and reimagine multilingual and multicultural teacher education through reflective practice and professional development across cultures. It is based on research that identifies and examines teachers' knowledge of culturally relevant teaching (CRT) practices in two elementary classrooms, one in China and one in the United States, in order to strengthen understanding of features and relationships of CRT and adaptive expertise (AE). In particular, the research investigated teachers' practices, perceptions and thinking in the context of CRT, as well as the perceptions of culture circles in each setting.

In preparation for launching this research, reflection on recent studies was needed. *Preschool in Three Cultures*, along with the more recent *Preschool in Three Cultures Revisited* (Tobin, 2019; Tobin et al., 1989; Tobin et al., 2009), served as the foundation of the research design to address our research questions. Mariana Souto-Manning's (2010) work (*Freire, Teaching, and Learning: Culture Circles Across Contexts*) helped to further develop the methodology as the data collection approach. The work of Annette Lareau (2011) provided additional contexts to inform about teacher education, family engagement, reflective practice, and considerations for a range of social identifiers. Cochran-Smith and Lytle's (2009) *Inquiry as Stance* was also leveraged with the intent of keeping practitioner experience as a central focus of the work and end product.

CONCEPTUAL FRAMEWORK

In this study, we believe that the education of children in schools, especially in urban areas, requires a theoretical framework of cultural pluralism. Multicultural education and culturally relevant pedagogy are two such perspectives that provide educators a framework to support them in working with the diverse cultures of students and families.

Research on multicultural education has demonstrated its effectiveness in explicitly addressing identity development among youth. As well, the practices of engaging youth in experiential learning and open dialogue have shown positive changes in students' perceptions of others, academic achievement, and self-esteem (Gordon, 2005; Henderson & Wilcox, 1998; Motti-Stefanidi & Masten, 2013; Oyserman & Destin, 2010). Hawley and Jackson (1995) found that racial attitudes and interracial behaviors can be improved through strategies that are a meaningful and significant part of the teacher's curriculum. They concluded that educators play a fundamental role in multicultural education and true progress requires supplemental training for classroom teachers and the opportunity for them to reflect on their experiences.

Culturally relevant teaching is a term that Gloria Ladson-Billings created to describe "a pedagogy that empowers students intellectually, socially, emotionally, and politically by using cultural references to impart knowledge, skills, and attitudes" (Ladson-Billings, 1994, pp. 17–18). Utilizing culturally relevant teaching practices essentially means that teachers create a connection between students' home and school lives, while still meeting the curricular requirements of their school system. Culturally relevant teaching leverages the backgrounds, knowledge, and experiences of students to inform the teacher's lessons and methodological approach.

Culturally relevant pedagogy is essential to multicultural education. Multicultural education is about acknowledging racial, socioeconomic, and ethnic differences instead of ignoring them. In order for multicultural education to work at the classroom level, teachers must employ effective teaching strategies (i.e., culturally relevant pedagogy). Culturally relevant teaching uses cultural knowledge, reference to prior experiences, and adaptation to the performance styles of diverse students to make learning more appropriate and effective for them. It teaches to and through the strengths of these students (Blazar, 2021; Gay, 2010; Motti-Stefanidi & Masten, 2013). By using cultural references to impart knowledge, skills, and attitudes, culturally relevant teaching acknowledges the role of students' backgrounds in their ability to frame and absorb knowledge. The outcome of it can be seen in students who are empowered intellectually, socially, emotionally, and politically (Blazar, 2021; Ladson-Billings, 2005, 2014). Culturally relevant teaching recognizes the value of each culture that a student brings into the classroom and bridges the gap between learning and teaching through reflective interaction between the teacher and their students. Acknowledging different learning approaches and frames of reference supports adaptive expertise and encourages students to leverage a variety of approaches in problem solving. Adaptive expertise, introduced by Hatano and Inagaki (1986), is a concept that incorporates a range of cognitive, motivational, and personality traits. A characteristic of adaptive expertise is the ability to apply knowledge effectively to new situations or unusual problems. Studies show that adaptive experts are able to demonstrate flexibility to invent new procedures that can result in better performance and technical troubleshooting (Carbonell et al., 2014; Holyoak, 1991). Hatano and Oura (2003) stated that school climates are often deficient in encouraging adaptive expertise and in promoting the sociocultural significance of content. They noted that while true adaptive expertise may not be a realistic goal for school learning, teaching toward the goal of adaptive expertise through the use of collaborative work, attempting to solve real-world problems, and presenting information to audiences will help to prepare for future competence (Hatano & Oura, 2003).

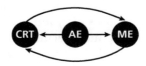

Figure 6.1 Conceptual framework for culturally relevant teaching.

Like a puzzle piece that completes a picture, adaptive expertise (AE) links to both multicultural education and culturally relevant teaching. Educators who use AE effectively in their teaching practices better leverage reflection, action, and judgment skills to move from theory to real-time teaching. For example, adaptive experts adopted new modalities during and beyond the COVID pandemic to ensure active interaction and engagement would still be expected as part of effective teaching and learning, using online synchronous tools such as zoom or hybrid mode combining synchronous and asynchronous modalities. Adaptive experts are open to transformative change in their practice. This means that when they discover the need to change a practice or process, they perceive it "not as a failure but, instead, as a success and an inevitable, continuous aspect of effective teaching" (Hammerness et al., 2005, p. 363). Critical components of adaptive expertise in the classroom are the ability to reflect on student responses and to understand and respond accordingly to the realities of classroom culture, in ways that place student learning at the forefront.

Siraj and Taggart (2014) found that teachers in schools deemed as "excellent" or "good" were more likely to personalize their students' learning experiences. They did this by being sensitive to the individual needs of the children in their classrooms and by using learning materials that were rich and varied. This is in comparison to the schools that were rated "very low," in which teacher detachment (distancing themselves from their pupils by staying at their desks, not providing feedback, not noticing behaviors, etc.) was high. As well, teachers in "excellent" schools were sensitive to the needs of the children and provided learning materials specifically chosen and modified for their students.

Recognizing and capitalizing on student experience and prior knowledge is a shift from traditional instructional practices of elementary school teachers that are often reflective of authoritarian power structures that model other work environments (Blazar, 2021; Sarason, 1990). For example, Manke (1997) explored how teachers arrange class time and space to control student behavior and promote learning. She described how the "authoritarian" fifth-grade teacher arranged her room in a way that discouraged students from moving. The exit was also "tightly controlled," and three of the most difficult students sat in "isolated seats" chosen by the teacher. Manke also explored how teachers can use structured activities to control student behavior. While power relationships can be enforced through setting and approach to pedagogy, it is important to note how they can also persist through identity and constructions of difference—and to understand how minority and/or majority group membership can play a significant role in those power dynamics (Delpit, 1988; Freire, 1970; McLaren, 1994).

Teachers need time to practice and reflect upon their development and their execution of curricular and pedagogical strategies to ensure the needs of students are met (Banks et al., 2001; Blazar, 2021; Ladson-Billings, 2005; White-Clark, 2005). Increased awareness and self-reflection can expose one's own biases and be an essential first step toward establishing a culturally responsive learning environment and reducing cultural bias in teaching (Blazar, 2021; Gay, 2010). Reflective practice, however, cannot be accomplished in a bubble. Feedback to and from others is critical to deepening one's worldview and cultural understanding (Hammerness et al., 2005).

IMPLEMENTING THE CONCEPTUAL FRAMEWORK IN RESEARCH DESIGN

In general, research design and methodology are formed by the nature of the specific problem to be studied, by the questions it raises, and by the type of end product desired (Creswell, 1998; Merriam, 1998). In this case, qualitative design was chosen leveraging *video-cued multivocal ethnography* to address research questions to examine and compare CRT practices in China and the U.S. through two classrooms (Tobin, 2019; Tobin et al., 2009; Tobin et al., 1989). *Video-cued multivocal ethnography* is a research method of using film with informant-participants to elicit explanations and responses to educational contexts that can reveal the cultural, linguistic, ethnic and sociopolitical variation in how people understand educational ideas, practices, policies, and relationships. By examining teachers' collective discourse and reflective responses about the videotaped teacher's thinking and instructional behaviors, this approach provides a way to capture and better understand each participant's personal and interpretive meanings and perspectives (Bogdan & Biklen, 2003; Erickson, 1986; Stake, 1995).

Qualitative methods for data collection and analysis including interviews, focus groups, observations, and culture circles (Freire, 1970, 1985; Souto-Manning, 2010) were used. Selective and purposeful sampling was used throughout the study to obtain deeper understanding of the phenomenon observed. Qualitative methodology was chosen because it is designed to "help researchers understand the attitudes and behaviors of people within their natural, social and cultural contexts" (Jacelon & O'Dell, 2005, as cited in Hill, 2013, p. 67; Marshall & Rossman, 2014). This context-sensitive approach suited the study because it promotes the use of the participants' environment, which has the potential to increase comfort level during initial meetings. With limited time at each school site, it was believed that this approach would help alleviate any initial anxiety participants may have and strengthen the researcher's lens on each school setting and their culture.

Data Sources

Qualitative data were collected through multiple sources to explore culture-rich contexts in China and the United States. The following section describes the purpose of each source and how data were collected using a variety of approaches and techniques.

Classroom Teacher Data

Two classroom teachers were the participants of the classroom level data. One classroom teacher was from a public school located in the east coast of China and the other was from a public school located in the east coast of the United States. The first author set up initial meetings and scheduled reviews with the two teachers whose classrooms were going to be videotaped. During those meetings, the first author gathered information to better plan and organize for the classroom observations and videotaping sessions. A bilingual educator who was proficient in both Chinese and English was the interpreter for the observations and meetings in China.

The researchers observed individual teachers' classrooms over a one-week period prior to video-taping to better understand the general flow of the school day and to ensure students were used to the researchers' presence in the room. The final day included a full day of observation and video recording. Throughout the week, notes were taken to better organize for the observation date.

Once videotaping was completed for each observation, the researchers and videographer edited each day's video down to 20–30 minutes and showed the edited tape to the teacher whose classroom was filmed. Using a series of prompts, the teacher was asked to share insights on how and why they had specific interaction with students. Data were collected through notes and audio recordings.

Culture Circle Data

To explore educators' perceptions of other teachers' culturally relevant teaching practices and to compare these in the United States and China, initial meetings with culture circle groups made up of teachers from the two schools in both countries were scheduled to build rapport and review the process for the video-cued multivocal process.

At their next meeting, participants were asked to view a series of videos showing the teacher in their school community and one from another school. These acted as prompts to generate responses and encourage reflection from teachers and administrators. Initial questions or prompts to begin the discussion were used; the generative themes that arose from participants then guided the conversation. Responses were audio recorded and field notes were taken during the process to document context and researcher observations.

It is impossible to detach the data in each culture circle, or from each classroom teacher, from the context of each school community (Yin, 1994). The holistic nature of this design demands a thorough understanding of the contexts in which data were collected.

Video

While video was taken of each classroom, it was not used as actual data, but instead as a prompt for discussion in culture circles. However, choices needed to be made about taping and editing that would impact what the culture circles viewed. An educational researcher with experience in video production was leveraged for taping and editing in both the United States and China.

Because one goal of the video was to promote dialogue, emotional and/or dramatic interactions were prioritized in taping. Since another goal was to provide comparability across the two cultures, the researchers attempted to record similar situations and placed precedence on those types of interactions as filming took place, particularly in the second school videotaped. In editing the video clips, interactions with the teacher that validated a range of cultural heritages, family structures, and learning styles that integrated multicultural resources and promoted adaptive expertise were prioritized.

Video-Cued Prompted Sessions

Video-cued sessions were conducted with the two teachers whose classes were videotaped. These sessions allowed the teacher to view their own classroom engagement (edited version) and provided insight into the typicality of the situation and the thought process behind the engagement. These sessions were audio-taped and used during the culture circles' video-cued sessions. Field notes were taken during the process to document context and observations.

Video-cued sessions were also conducted with the two culture circles. Here, the participants were asked to view videos produced of a teacher in their school and one from another school and country. These videos acted as a prompt for participant response and reflection. While initial prompts may have been used to trigger the discussion, generative themes from participants guided the conversation. As well, after the original reflection, responses from the teacher in the video were shared to provide their context and thought process. These comments may have prompted additional reflection and even a shift in understanding or perception from the culture circle. Responses were audio-recorded and field notes were taken during the process to document context and researcher observations. Potential prompts were developed to use in these sessions and protocol was established based on descriptions of the *Preschool in Three Cultures* model.

Field Notes

Field notes are written interpretations of what a researcher observes during data collection sessions (Bogdan & Biklen, 2003). Field notes reinforce research by making it possible to report on events in real time and incorporating details of the event in a contextualized form (Yin, 1994). In this study, most field notes were taken from each of the classroom observations over the 1-week period. The field notes were summarized into brief statements by two categories: descriptive (note taking) and reflective (note making; Creswell, 1998). These brief statements were developed into more detailed, descriptive accounts of observations made during those sessions (Bogdan & Biklen, 2003). Summaries of the field notes provided additional information to help the researchers generate discussion prompts in follow up meetings and the culture circles.

Audio Recordings

Digital voice recorders were used to record both culture circle sessions. Audio recordings of the two culture circles provided researchers with the opportunity to revisit these sessions and aided in bringing attention to anything that may have been missed. This was especially important for the current study because two languages were involved. The researchers listened to all English recordings several times before reviewing the transcripts to verify the accuracy of the transcriptions. The translator did the same for all Chinese recordings and transcripts. Erickson (1986) believed that audio recorders are less obtrusive in these smaller settings and allow for a more thorough report of events than could be represented through field notes alone.

Ultimately, the data collected provided a rich source of perspectives on two teachers' classroom environments and teaching methods. It further amplified the need to better understand the interplay and connective tissue for multicultural education, AE and culturally relevant teaching, and for this study to be replicated.

Summary of Findings

The data from multiple sources revealed the nature of culturally relevant teaching practices that recognize the importance of including students' cultural references in all aspects of learning. Instructional practices representative of culturally relevant teaching were used by teachers in both classroom settings. Specifically, evidence was identified in the following approaches from both the United States and China classrooms: (a) fostered positive perspectives on parents and families, (b) messaged high expectations, (c) promoted learning within the context of culture, (d) used student-centered instruction, (e) leveraged culturally mediated instruction, (f) reshaped the curriculum, and (g) practiced using teacher as facilitator.

LESSONS LEARNED

Recommendations for Scholarship

Multicultural Education

Findings recognized a gap in teachers' discussion around identifiers linked to race and ethnicity in both the United States and China. Effective multicultural education must consider the broader socio-political factors that impact students' success or failure in the classroom (Nieto, 1996). This study revealed that culture circle participants in both settings repeatedly reflected and discussed the differences observed in the socio-political aspects of each culture (i.e., the collective versus the individual). Collectivism and individualism are known to deeply permeate cultures, including classroom settings, and the attention given to the topic warrants additional examination around its potential impact on teaching practices and student achievement in both countries. One difference was discerned between the two culture circle conversations that should also be examined. In China, the discourse on the topic appeared to be from a place of inquiry, whereas participants in the United States were perceived by the researcher as coming from a place of judgment, then moving to curiosity. For example, culture circle participants shared their perceptions on where they saw teachers acting as facilitators in their classrooms. In China, there were more questions on how the observed U.S. teacher was able to provide small groups instruction the way she did, allowing students to lead and facilitate their own learning at stations. In the United States, the participants wanted to understand more about the differences of the two cultures and how to correlate some of the culture changes in the United States as potential opportunities.

Critical Reflective Practice Using Video-Cued Ethnography

Effective culturally responsive teachers continually reflect on and improve their practices. Findings from interviews and culture circle discussions showed considerable interest and enthusiasm around the use of video for similar reflection and learning, specifically as it relates to self-reflection and cross-cultural study.

After the U.S. teacher observed herself and students on video, she immediately began to reflect on her approach and with no prompting, verbalizing alternative tactics. Further research on the use of video reflection for teacher development is recommended.

Culture circle participants in both settings were fully engaged watching the video prompts. After footage ended, they immediately began engaging and asking questions, even asking why we don't film classroom settings more. The classroom teachers asked if they could view the classroom videos from the other country. Video is a powerful and meaningful tool for reflection and intervention, especially in the post pandemic era. Its use is becoming more prevalent as advances in technology bring about more accessible and cost-efficient tools for recording. Even some of the language might suggest the perceived differences between cultures. For example, the Chinese circles continued to refer to China as "our China," suggesting a more collective goal versus an individual goal, which could have implications on how expectations are shared and how classroom learning happens. Additional research on the use of video-cued ethnography and collaborative video-cued narrative for reflective practice should be pursued and is recommended for comparative research across cultures. Further study and advancement of these methods would aid in demonstrating its broad potential for teachers' reflective practice and development.

Recommendations for Practice

Practitioner Reflection and Inquiry

Culture circle participants in both countries expressed enthusiasm about the culture circle model, the dialogue it promoted, and the camaraderie they experienced. As well, U.S. teachers conveyed a need for greater connection with their colleagues to further develop as practitioners. Based on these findings, teachers should implement culture circles with colleagues in their schools. Culture circles create space in which individuals can question current realities and leverage their existing knowledge as valued contributors. Culture circles are generated by the dialogue and themes that come from the participants, so they make a powerful tool for reflection, ideation, and empowerment. Because collaborative time is limited in the United States, culture circles should be tested at a smaller scale using classroom artifacts as prompts for discussion. In China, where more time is allotted for reflection and collaboration, this model could be broadened more deeply. Newly formed culture circles should strive to include teachers from across grade levels and subject areas. Practitioner culture circles can serve as a pilot for educators. As comfort increases, teachers in both settings can adapt the model for their classrooms, further building upon CRT practices.

Throughout this study, all teacher participants in the United States expressed interest in observing their colleagues more and showed concern about their ability to prioritize the time. Based on the need to further increase opportunities for reflection in the United States, teachers should adopt some of the practices used in China including: (a) inviting others in to observe their classrooms on a regular basis, requesting constructive feedback for reflection; (b) promoting a growth mindset by asking to informally observe others in and across subjects and grades; and (c) applying learnings to the classroom, then testing, adapting, and iterating on new practices and models.

Culturally Relevant Teaching-Related Professional Development
Teaching methods that connect with students' experiences and promote understanding of other cultures are associated with better academic outcomes. Additionally, encouraging students' knowledge and understanding of their own culture is connected to increased engagement and positive self-esteem. Study findings from both the United States and China showed little evidence supporting teachers' use of culturally relevant teaching practices in relation to positive perspectives on parents and families, valuing students' lived experiences, and reshaping the curriculum. In both settings, educators racial and ethnic identities were not reflective of the broader communities they served, and there was no evidence of discussion about race, ethnicity, or systemic inequities throughout observations, interviews, and culture circle sessions. To better leverage these practices effectively, and address the identified gaps, teachers in both countries need to increase their knowledge of ME and culturally relevant teaching so they can mitigate bias, develop stronger skill sets to connect and relate to students and families of all backgrounds, and reflect on the curriculum. Teachers in the United States and China should: (a) connect with their students, learn about their cultural backgrounds, and personalize instruction; (b) teach about cultural diversity even when the class is not diverse (this should be prioritized in China); (c) acknowledge and openly discuss and reflect on systemic inequities; and (d) advocate for professional growth and development in culturally relevant teaching.

CONCLUSION

Culturally relevant teaching is a powerful method that permeates the classroom environment increasing student connectedness, engagement, and achievement. When students experience a sense of belonging, it has the transformative capacity to increase self-esteem and strengthen self-identity. This research study demonstrated how teachers leverage and perceive culturally relevant teaching practices in their schools.

The findings provide support for the effectiveness of culturally relevant teaching in everyday classrooms, despite the diverse challenges faced by countries in different parts of a changing world. Taken together, these findings demonstrate and compare the ways in which elementary school teachers in China and the United States practice and perceive culturally relevant teaching. As the study was grounded in a framework linking adaptive expertise, multicultural education and culturally relevant teaching, the resulting assertions can influence adoption and differentiation of teaching strategies that better leverage reflection, inquiry, action, and judgment skills to move from theory to real-time teaching. The following findings were revealed from the study: (a) differences in frequency and application of practices, (b) communication of high expectations across cultures, (c) lack of family and community partnership, (d) emphasis on culturally mediated instruction in the United States, and (e) ample time for collaboration and reflection in China.

The world continues to transform at a rapid pace, made even more evident by the global pandemic which resulted in the loss of millions and impacted the lives of so many more. Globalization is another transformation that comes with the growth of diverse populations, increasing the importance of teachers affirming students' identities across dimensions—including languaging and dynamically lingual identities. Thus, there is an even greater need to continue the examination of teachers' cultural competency and reflective practices. Utilizing comparative research across countries is certainly evident in areas like student achievement, curriculum, and evaluation. However, little emphasis has been placed on teacher preparation and effectiveness, particularly as it relates to multicultural education, culturally relevant teaching, and adaptive expertise. The need for comparison of research, policy, and best practices in these areas is critical for professional development of educators and their impact on students' identity development and academic achievement around the world.

REFERENCES

Banks, J. A., Cookson, P., Gay, G., Hawley, W. D., Jordan Irvine, J., Nieto, S., Schofield, J. W., & Stephan, W. G. (2001). *Diversity within unity: Essential principles for teaching and learning in a multicultural society*. Center for Multicultural Education, University of Washington.

Banks, J. A., & McGee Banks, C. A. (2004). *Handbook for multicultural education*. Jossey-Bass.

Banks, J. A., & McGee Banks, C. A. (2012). *Multicultural education: Issues and perspectives*. John Wiley & Sons.

Blazar, D. (2021). *Teachers of color, culturally responsive teaching and student outcomes: Experimental evidence from the random assignment of teachers to classes* [Ed working paper no. 21-501]. Annenberg Institute for School Reform at Brown University.

Bogdan, R. C., & Biklen, S. K. (2003). *Qualitative research for education: An introduction to theory and methods* (4th ed.). Allyn & Bacon.

Carbonell, K. B., Stalmeijer, R. E., Könings, K. D., Segers, M., & van Merriënboer, J. (2014). How experts deal with novel situations: A review of adaptive expertise. *Educational Research Review, 12*, 14–29.

Clunies-Ross, P., Little, E., & Kienhuis, M. (2008). Self-reported and actual use of proactive and reactive classroom management strategies and their relationship with teacher stress and student behavior. *Educational Psychology, 28*(6), 693–710.

Cochran-Smith, M., & Lytle, S. L. (2009). *Inquiry as stance: Practitioner research for the next generation.* Teachers College Press.

Cole, R. (2008). *Educating everybody's children: Diverse teaching strategies for diverse learners.* Association for Curriculum and Supervision Development.

Creswell, J. W. (1998). *Qualitative inquiry and research design.* SAGE.

Darling-Hammond, L. (2006). *Powerful teacher education: Lessons from exemplary programs.* Wiley.

Delpit, L. (1988). The silenced dialogue: Power and pedagogy in educating other people's children. *Harvard Educational Review, 58*(3), 280–298.

Erickson, F. (1986). Qualitative methods in research on teaching. In M. C. Wittrock (Ed.), *Handbook of research on teaching* (3rd ed., pp. 119–161). Macmillan.

Freire, P. (1970). *Pedagogy of the oppressed.* Seabury.

Freire, P. (1985). *The politics of education: Culture, power, and liberation.* Bergin & Garvin.

Gay, G. (2010). *Culturally responsive teaching: Theory, research, and practice.* Teachers College Press.

Gordon, E. W. (2005). The idea of supplementary education. In E. Gordon, B. Bridglall, & A. Meroe (Eds.), *Supplementary education: The hidden curriculum of high academic achievement.* Rowman & Littlefield.

Hammerness, K., Darling-Hammond, L., Bransford, J., Berliner, D., Cochran-Smith, M., McDonald, M., & Kenneth, Z. (2005). How teachers learn and develop. In L. Darling-Hammond & J. Bransford (Eds.), *Preparing teachers for a changing world: What teachers should learn and be able to do.* Jossey-Bass.

Hatano, G., & Inagaki, K. (1986). Two courses of expertise. In H. Stevenson, H. Azuma, & K. Hakuta (Eds.), *Child development and education in Japan* (pp. 262–272). W. H. Freeman.

Hatano, G., & Oura, Y. (2003). Reconceptualizing school learning using insight from expertise research. *Educational Researcher, 32*(8), 26–29.

Hawley, W. D., & Jackson, A. (1995). *Toward a common destiny: Improving race and ethnic relations in America.* Jossey-Bass.

Hayutin, A. M. (2007). Global demographic shifts. *PREA Quarterly.*

Henderson, A., & Wilcox, S. (1998). A+ strategies for strong partnering. *Schools in the Middle,* (November/December), 32–38.

Hill, Antonia L. (2013) *Culturally responsive teaching: An investigation of effective practices for African American learners* (Doctoral dissertation; Paper 353). Loyola University.

Holyoak, K. J. (1991). Symbolic connectionism: Toward third-generation theories of expertise. In K. A. Ericsson & J. Smith (Eds.), *Toward a general theory of expertise: Prospects and limits* (pp. 301–335). Cambridge University Press.

Jacelon, C. S., & O'Dell, K. K. (2005). Uses of qualitative research: So what good is it? *American Urological Association Allied, 25*(6), 471–473.

Kwok, A. (2021). Managing classroom management preparation in teacher education. *Teachers and Teaching, 27*, 1–17.

Ladson-Billings, G. (1994). *The dreamkeepers: Successful teaching for African American students.* Jossey-Bass.

Ladson-Billings, G. (2005). *Culturally relevant teaching: A special issue of theory into practice.* Routledge.

Ladson-Billings, G. (2014) Culturally Relevant Pedagogy 2.0: A.K.A. the remix. *Harvard Educational Review, 84*(1), 74–84.

Lareau, A. (2011). *Unequal childhoods: Class, race, and family life.* University of California Press.

Manke, M. (1997). *Classroom power relations: Understanding student-teacher interaction.* Lawrence Erlbaum.

Marshall, C., & Rossman, G. (2014). *Designing qualitative research.* SAGE.

McLaren, P. (1994). *Life in schools: An introduction to critical pedagogy in the foundations of education.* Longman.

Merrett, F., & Wheldall, K. (1993). How do teachers learn to manage classroom behavior? A study of teachers' opinions about their initial training with special reference to classroom behavior management. *Educational Studies, 19*, 91–106.

Merriam, S. B. (1998). *Qualitative research and case study applications in education.* Jossey-Bass.

Motti-Stefanidi, F., & Masten, A. S. (2013). School success and school engagement of immigrant children and adolescents. *European Psychologist, 18*, 126–135.

Nieto, S. (1996). *Affirming diversity: The sociopolitical context of multicultural education* (2nd ed.). Longman.

Oyserman, D., & Destin, M. (2010). Identity-based motivation: Implications for intervention. *The Counseling Psychologist, 38*, 1001–1043.

Reinke, W. M., Stormont, M., Herman, K. C., Puri, R., & Goel, N. (2011). Supporting children's mental health in schools: Teacher perceptions of needs, roles, and barriers. School *Psychology Quarterly, 26*, 1–13.

Sarason, S. B. (1990). *The predictable failure of educational reform: Can we change course before it's too late?* Jossey-Bass.

Siraj, I., & Taggart, B. (2014). *Exploring effective pedagogy in primary schools: Evidence from research.* Pearson.

Souto-Manning, M. (2010). *Freire, teaching, and* learning. Peter Lang Publishing.

Stake, R. E. (1995). *The art of case study research.* SAGE.

Tillery, A. D., Varjas, K., Meyers, J., & Smith Collins, A. (2010). General education teachers' perceptions of behavior management and intervention strategies. *Journal of Positive Behavior, 12*(2), 86–102.

Tobin, J. (2019). The origins of the video-cued multivocal ethnographic method. *Anthropology & Education Quarterly, 50*(3), 255–269.

Tobin, J. J., Hsueh, Y., & Karasawa, M. (2009). *Preschool in three cultures revisited.* The Chicago University Press.

Tobin, J. J., Wu, D. Y. H., & Davidson, D. H. (1989). *Preschool in three cultures.* Yale University Press.

United Nations. (2019). *World population prospects: The 2019 revision.* The United Nations.

White-Clark, R. (2005). Training teachers to succeed in a multicultural classroom. *Education Digest, 70*(8), 23–26.

Yin, R. K. (1994). *Case study research: Design and methods* (2nd ed.). SAGE.

CHAPTER 7

MAPPING A MULTILINGUAL FUTURE

Navigating Uncertainty With Equitable Pedagogies

Lourdes Cardozo-Gaibisso
Mississippi State University

Ruth Harman
University of Georgia

Max Vazquez Dominguez
University of North Georgia

Cory Buxton
Oregon State University

ABSTRACT

This final chapter explores the changes in multilingual education catalyzed by the COVID-19 pandemic and its aftermath. It presents findings from six diverse studies across different countries, showcasing the challenges and innovations arising from the crisis. Authors from each of the chapters delve into instructional strategies, curriculum adaptations, and assessment practices, emphasizing equity and accessibility for diverse learners. They advocate for a reimagining of education that prioritizes the needs of multilingual and multicultural communities, utilizing digital and multimodal resources. Through self-reflection and empirical studies, contributors stress the importance of context and adaptation, proposing pedagogical innovations that honor linguistic and cultural diversity. Ultimately, this chapter urges collective action to embrace equitable pedagogies and shape an inclusive educational landscape for all learners.

As we write this final chapter, echoes of the world health pandemic still resonate if a bit more faintly than in the throes of the disaster. Educators and policy makers find themselves standing on the precipice of a new era in multilingual education, one that has been shaped by devastating personal and professional challenges during COVID-19 and also by the profound transformations in the way language education is perceived and carried out. The contributors to this volume are all part of this radical change to our field, showing through their conceptual and empirical studies the resilience and creativity of educators in the face of adversity.

In the aftermath of what we now see as a time of global disruption, the education community worldwide faces many challenges both at the individual and collective level. The online and distance learning experiences included in this book highlight varied instructional strategies, curriculum adaptations, and assessment practices as tools to change and improve reality while respecting and honoring the unique experiences of each multilingual and multicultural community. The six chapters document the multifaceted strengths and challenges that emerged during and after the pandemic in Uruguay, Colombia, China, and the United States, giving readers the opportunity to analyze and understand the reconceptualization of online instruction, through the use of digital and multimodal resources which were harnessed to fully engage multilingual students in optimal and equitable learning contexts. The chapters also provide the reader with the opportunity to reflect on the dynamic landscape in education and to use and adapt the tools and recommendations for other contexts.

As chapter book authors described their pedagogical innovations, we repeatedly found ourselves reflecting on the notion of "competing priorities" as it echoed through the pages and continues to challenge stakeholders to discern what could and could not be done within the realms of human, financial, and logistic capacity worldwide. This challenge, while daunting, keeps presenting itself as an opportunity for a collective reimagining of education—one that prioritizes equity, accessibility, and the diverse needs of multilingual students beyond the individual efforts.

Each chapter, with its specific theoretical positionings and perspectives on societal power dynamics, underscores the interconnected topics explored in multilingual and multicultural settings. From instructional strategies and curriculum adaptations to in-service and pre-service teacher education practices, and from classroom-based pedagogical innovations to assessment methodologies, the narrative weaves together a tapestry of the challenges and innovations that shaped, and continue to shape, the recent landscape of multilingual teaching. In this light, we encourage readers to try adopting these approaches, adapting them to start new iterations or to take some pieces and experiment plugging them into a different theoretical positioning, perspective, and/or methodology. These chapters highlight the importance of context, and thus, the need to adapt all practices to the unique demands of each multilingual and multicultural landscape.

As we move through these chapters, we can see authors using self-reflection, theoretical innovation, and empirical studies that relate to their digital, language, multimodal and assessment practices. Luciana de Oliveira and Larisa Olesova in the first chapter provide us with important details of their self-study of an ESOL methods course that was moved online during the pandemic. They provide helpful and detailed information about the competencies that multilingual educators need to develop to ensure that their asynchronous online courses include interactive, multimodal, and effective strategies in all domains of instruction, including assessment and evaluation (Martin et al., 2019; Olesova & de Oliveira, 2015). They encourage readers to take up the mantle, designing and implementing similar types of courses that support multilingual learners in holistic ways.

In their chapter, Carla Meskill, Guo Dogni, Fang Wang, and Wuri Kusumastuti discuss their longitudinal case study of two elementary English as a foreign language (EFL) teachers in China as they transition from their teaching online during their 3-month lockdown to a return to their regular classrooms after restrictions had been lifted. The authors discuss how the affordances of online teaching, especially through innovative digital ways (Meskill et al., 2020) they could tailor, manage, and extend instruction, supported them in continuing the same practices when they returned to face-to-face instruction. They urge educators to become familiar with the affordances of online instruction as a way to develop their classroom teaching in innovative and impactful ways.

Connected also to online instruction but with a focus on assessment practices, Gabriel Díaz Maggioli provides readers with details of a design-based research project he developed with student teachers in a Uruguayan teacher education program. To challenge onerous issues related to online assessment including questions of authenticity and identity protection, and equity (Elzainy et al., 2020), the author supported the student teachers in developing theoretical and empirical understanding of these issues. In similar ways, Maria Eugenia Lozano's chapter provides readers with details of her online university assessment practices that she and her colleagues developed during the pandemic. Specifically, she provides readers with information about their formative assessments that focused more on students' organic processes of using grammar, vocabulary, and cultural content as opposed to fixed measurement related to language and grammar accuracy. The chapter includes faculty and student critical reflections on such assessment practices and how they shaped their language learning and teaching during times of uncertainty.

In their chapter, Wilder Escobar-Almeciga, Deisy Caviedes-Cadena, and Fabián Jiménez discuss the challenges that teachers and students faced in Colombian English as a foreign language (EFL) classrooms once all instruction migrated to online context. To support readers in understanding the challenges for an undergraduate bilingual teaching program in this era, the authors provide innovative and thought-provoking reflections and actions that emerged from their negotiation of the complex issues related to equity, access, and community. Most importantly, the authors discuss their deep commitment to democratic, communicative, and ethical values that they solidified during COVID-19 and have continued to develop (Escobar-Alméciga & Brutt-Griffler, 2022).

In the final chapter, Alicia Thompson and Yaoying Xu provide readers with a description of the video-cued ethnography study and culture circles they conducted in elementary schools in China and the United States. They discuss how the use of cultural circle practices (Freire, 1970, 1985; Souto-Manning, 2010) supported participants in thinking about their lived experiences and in developing agency as related to their teaching and learning practices. Based on their study of these two environments, the authors recommend that culture circle practices be adopted in school-wide programs so that educators can deepen their understanding of multicultural education and culturally sustaining curriculum design.

As editors of this book, our engagement with these six distinct studies have augmented our sense of optimism, which initially sparked our interest in conducting this work in the first place. As evidenced in these studies, the trials and tribulations of the pandemic have resulted in a metamorphosis of sorts, a time where we rethink how we map a multilingual future that must be different from what it once was, pushing the boundaries of what we once believed to be possible in education. This mapping of lessons learned can guide the way towards a more resilient, inclusive, and equitable future for multilingual learners and educators. However, we also need to be aware of the limitations of just focusing on individual efforts in our pursuit of an equitable multilingual agenda for an uncertain world. Instead, this mapping should help us to keep sight of our role as multicultural and multilingual advocates at many levels (e.g., state and national) where policies continue to favor monolingualism (e.g., English-only policies prevalent in many states in the United States). As much as possible, we need to develop and sustain dynamic online and face to face classrooms where all languages, cultures, and ethnicities are incorporated in curriculum design and instruction. The seismic shifts in educational practices forced upon us by the pandemic have not only exposed the structural issues entrenched in our societies but have also unveiled the potential for transformative change. As we stand at the precipice of a post-pandemic future, this need for equitable pedagogies has never been more pronounced.

This final chapter serves as a reflective point—a summit from which we survey the landscape we have navigated thus far and glimpse the horizon of possibilities that awaits us. The theme of equitable pedagogies resonates through the narrative of the book, reminding us that our journey is not just about overcoming challenges but about creating an educational future that is inclusive, accessible, and responsive to the diverse needs of our multilingual learners. In other words, as educators we need to be proactive in solving problems, building new ideas, and reinforcing the hope in multilingual classrooms where multilingual communities are represented and supported. Equitable pedagogies need to be the guiding principles shaping our educational endeavors, ensuring that no learner (e.g., in-service teacher, pre-service teacher, student) is forgotten, regardless of their linguistic or cultural background.

As we close this book, let it be a call to action—a call to educators, policy makers, and advocates of education everywhere. The multilingual future we seek is within reach, but the journey continues. Together, let us forge ahead, navigating uncertainty with the unwavering commitment to equitable pedagogies, and in doing so, let us shape an educational landscape that truly serves humanity.

REFERENCES

Elzainy, A., El Sadik, A., & Al Abdulmonem, W. (2020). Experience of e-learning and online assessment during the COVID-19 pandemic at the College of Medicine, Qassim University. *Journal of Taibah University Medical Sciences 15*(6), 256–462. https://doi.org/10.1016/j.jtumed.2020.09.005

Escobar-Alméciga, W., & Brutt-Griffler, J. (2022). Multimodal communication in an early childhood bilingual education setting: A social semiotic interaction analysis. *Íkala Revista de Lenguaje y Cultura, 27*(1), 85–106.

Freire, P. (1970). *Pedagogy of the oppressed.* Seabury.

Freire, P. (1985). *The politics of education: Culture, power, and liberation.* Bergin & Garvin.

Martin, F., Budhrani, K., Kumar, S., & Ritzhaupt, A. (2019). Award-winning faculty online teaching practices: Roles and competencies. *Online Learning, 23*(1), 184–205. https://doi.org/10.24059/olj.v23i1.1329

Meskill, C., Anthony, N., & Sadykova, G. (2020). Teaching languages online: Professional vision in the making. *Language Learning & Technology, 24*(3), 160–175. http://hdl.handle.net/10125/44745

Olesova, L., & de Oliveira, L. C. (2015). Using embedded audio feedback for formative assessment purposes in teaching about English language learners. In S. Koc, P. Wachira, & X. Liu, (Eds.), *Assessment in online and blended learning environments* (pp. 125–142). Information Age Publishing.

Souto-Manning, M. (2010). *Freire, teaching, and learning.* Peter Lang Publishing.

ABOUT THE CONTRIBUTORS

Alicia R. Thompson is a researcher and practitioner whose professional experiences in teaching, leadership and consulting in K–12, higher education and corporate America have fueled her research endeavors of examining culturally responsive practices. Dr. Thompson's work demonstrates her belief in practitioners' influence on underserved communities for whom she passionately advocates.

Carla Meskill is professor emerita, Department of Educational Theory and Practice, State University of New York, Albany. Since the first desktop computers emerged in the 1980s, she was at the forefront of design, research and practical training in how digital screens can best be made use of in education. She established and directed three technology research centers at major universities, served as a research and design consultant for a number of industries and institutions, authored and led nine federal grants in instructional technology research and implementation and shared her work around the world. Her publications include numerous books and research articles on digital screen mediation in classrooms, in online instruction, and in educator professional development.

Cory Buxton is a professor of science education at Oregon State University. His research fosters more equitable and justice-centered science learning opportunities for all students, and especially for multilingual learners, by bringing together teacher professional learning and family engagement experiences in both school-based and out of school settings. Buxton's research has been funded by the U.S. National Science Foundation, the U.S. Department of Education, and by several private foundations.

Lorena Caviedes-Cadena holds an MA in applied linguistics to TEFL from Universidad Distrital Francisco José de Caldas, and a BEd in philology and languages–English from Universidad Nacional de Colombia. She currently works as a full time professor for the Philology and languages program from Universidad Nacional de Colombia, and is an active member of the PROFILE research group from the same institution. Her research interests are focused on issues related to social justice, interculturality, gender, and power relations in multilingual educational contexts.

Gabriel Díaz Maggioli is the director of the graduate diploma in English language teaching and faculty in the graduate programs at the Institute of Education at Universidad ORT Uruguay. His area of research is teacher education within a sociocultural perspective. He has shared his theory and praxis with colleagues in the Americas, Europe, the Middle East, and Asia. He is a Tier 1 certified researcher in Uruguay's National Research and Innovation Agency.

Dongni Guo, MEd, is a doctoral student of educational theory and practice, State University of New York, Albany. Her research focuses on Language teacher professional development, with a particular emphasis on the effective utilization of technology and digital resources to enhance teacher–student–parent interactions and collaborations in online learning environments.

Fabián Benavides Jiménez is a doctoral student in the PhD program in social studies at Universidad Jorge Tadeo Lozano, Bogotá, Colombia; MA in literary studies from Universidad Santo Tomás, Bogotá, Colombia; BEd in Spanish and foreign languages from Universidad Pedagógica Nacional, Bogotá, Colombia. He is an associate professor at Universidad El Bosque, Bogotá, Colombia.

Fang Wang, MS, a doctoral student in educational theory and practice at the State University of New York, Albany, specializes in the fields of online language education and computer-assisted language learning and teaching. Her primary research interest lies in examining engagement patterns and learning processes among students involved in online language learning activities.

Larisa Olesova is a clinical assistant professor in the School of Teaching and Learning at the University of Florida. Her research focuses on distance education, specifically asynchronous online learning environments. Other areas of research and practice include aspects of online presence, the community of inquiry (CoI), instructional strategies and best practices in online teaching. She has authored or co-authored 1 book, 12 peer-reviewed journal articles and 11 book chapters to date in addition to other publications and have presented over 30 sessions at regional, state, national, and international conferences.

Luciana C. de Oliveira (PhD) is associate dean for academic affairs and graduate studies in the School of Education and professor in the Department of Teaching and Learning at Virginia Commonwealth University. Her research focuses on issues related to teaching multilingual learners at the elementary and secondary levels, including the role of language in learning the content areas. Dr. de Oliveira has authored or edited 28 books and has over 200 publications in various outlets. She has over 30 years of teaching experience in the field of TESOL. She served in the presidential line (2017–2020), served as president in 2018–2019, and was a member of the Board of Directors (2013–2016) of TESOL International Association. She was the very first Latina to serve as president of TESOL.

Lourdes Cardozo Gaibisso is an assistant professor of TESOL and linguistics in the Department of English at Mississippi State University, and director of the SL4E: Science Literacy for Equity Research Collaboratory at the MSU Social Science Research Center. Lourdes specializes in systemic functional linguistics, science literacy for minoritized populations, culturally and linguistically sustaining pedagogies, and TESOL.

Magdalena Pando is an associate professor of bilingual education in the Department of Teaching and Learning at Southern Methodist University. Her work bridges the field of teacher education, science disciplinary language and literacy, culturally relevant education informed by sociocultural theory, systemic functional linguistics, sociolinguistics, constructivist theory, and second language acquisition. Her research focuses on model-based inquiry methods in STEM education, teacher preparation and professional development. Recent research interests include investigating teachers' use of generative artificial intelligence natural language processing models as pedagogical tools in language education.

María Eugenia Lozano, EdD in education from the University of Massachusetts-Amherst. Dr. Lozano joined Barnard College's faculty in 2010. Previously, she taught at Columbia University, University of Massachusetts, Amherst College, Holyoke Community College, and Washington State University. Professor Lozano's research interests include second language acquisition, language maintenance among immigrants, and the use of technology for language teaching. At Barnard she teaches beginner, intermediate, and advanced Spanish languages courses.

Max Vazquez Dominguez is an associate professor at the University of North Georgia. His work promotes science and engineering education in elementary and middle grades and supports preservice teachers in collaborating with Latine/Latinx/Latino families and their multilingual children. He focuses on assemblage theory and culturally sustaining pedagogies to guide his work in the community.

Ruth Harman is a professor in the Department of Language and Literacy Education at the University of Georgia. Her research and teaching focus on issues related to immigration, multilingual education, and youth civic engagement. Over the past two decades she has used performance and improvisation in her work with teachers, youth, and community members to interrogate and disrupt normative minoritizing discourses. She has published in three overlapping areas related to this focus: critical systemic functional linguistics (SFL), critical performative pedagogy (CPP), and youth participatory action research.

Wilder Yesid Escobar-Almeciga PhD in foreign and second language education from University at Buffalo, NY; MA in applied linguistics to TEFL from Universidad Distrital Francisco José de Caldas, Bogotá, Colombia; BA in business administration from Simpson University, Redding, CA. He is a full professor at Universidad El Bosque, Bogotá, Colombia.

Wuri Kusumastuti, MEd, MS, ABD, is a PhD candidate in the Department of Educational Theory and Practice at the State University of New York, Albany. Her research centers on informal language learning in online spaces, with a specific focus on the activities of autonomous language learners engaged in practice within the digital realm. Her recent work delves into the ways autonomous language learners actively seek second language interaction through various social media platforms, aiming to enhance both their receptive and productive language skills in the target language. This research contributes valuable insights into the evolving landscape of language acquisition in the context of contemporary online informal environments.

Yaoying Xu is a professor in early childhood special education of the Counseling and Special Education Department at Virginia Commonwealth University. Dr. Xu's research interests focus on social aspects of children with culturally and linguistically diverse backgrounds and how social interaction affects children's academic performance. Her current research examines the effects of adult-scaffolded peer tutoring on young English learners' social and language skills. Additionally, her research intends to investigate children's social skills as mediators and home language as moderators in young dual language learners' language and literacy skills. Dr. Xu has been a principal investigator or co-principal investigator of numerous nationally or state funded grant projects generating over $15 million. Dr. Xu has published nearly 90 peer-reviewed journal articles and book chapters in addition to over 200 presentations at national and international professional conferences.

Printed in the USA
CPSIA information can be obtained
at www.ICGtesting.com
CBHW052348191024
15920CB00003B/6